Toscan

Giuliano Cenci

The Secrets of Florence

Fascinating facts, amusing anecdotes, titbits,
and hidden truths about Florence's greatest artists
and monuments, illustrating the wit, guile,
and ingenuity of the true Florentine spirit

sarnus

Author's note

This little book has no pretensions to be a tourist guide or, still less, a treatise on art history. It's something else entirely that seeks to get to the heart of the ancient spirit of Florence, something that will enliven the visit to the city and can then be taken home as a rather special little souvenir.

The photos in the illustrations are by Elena Cenci, except where otherwise indicated.

www.sarnus.it

1st Italian edition: June 2008
Reprints: January 2009, December 2009, December 2010, December 2012, December 2014, September 2016, February 2019, March 2022, Dicembre 2023.
1st English edition: *The Secrets of Florence*, Sarnus, Florence, January 2025 (translation: Aelmuire Helen Cleary)

© 2025 Leonardo Libri srl
Via Livorno, 8/32 - 50142 Firenze - Tel. 055 73787
info@leonardolibri.com - www.leonardolibri.com

ISBN 978-88-563-0344-5

PREFACE

Florence is no longer the 'big' city that it was in the past. Today it's a medium-sized city with a population of around 367,500, including approximately 59,000 foreigners (data for February 2024), although it continues to be famous all over the world for its vast wealth of artistic treasures – paintings, sculpture and architecture – from all periods.

Although in the past Florence did not extend over such a large area, it was nevertheless a great and powerful city, dominant in both military and commercial terms and widely feared and respected. Eight hundred years ago Florence had fewer than 50,000 inhabitants but, almost as though it had inherited the invincibility of the ancient legions of imperial Rome, its army was the most powerful not only in Italy but possibly in the whole of Europe. It was feared by kings, emperors, and lords, and when it waged war was sure to return victorious and bearing rich booty.

As a financial and commercial power Florence had no equals. Suffice it to say that it was the first city to mint its own money, in a gesture of proud and daring appropriation of authority that was also a clear declaration of independence from the German imperial laws that Italy was subject to at the time. The first coin minted in Florence – also known as the silver *grosso* – was thick and solid and made of pure silver. On one side it bore the figure of John the Baptist, the patron saint of the city and on the other the lily that was the symbol of the city, which is why it was called a 'florin', the name by which it came to be known throughout the world. The first silver florin was struck in 1237, but Florence was far too proud a city to be content with a mere silver coin. So, in 1252 it struck the first florins made of the purest 24-carat gold! This was decidedly the most eloquent statement Florence could make about its wealth, power and greatness. Since the time of the Roman Empire no one had been able to flaunt such opulence, and even the emperors had rarely been able to stamp their images and names on gold. Instead, in Florence the precious metal streamed out of the mint, which was referred to as a 'spring of gold'. With a value that remained stable over time, the gold florin became a symbol of political prosperity and a guarantee of mercantile stability, and it conquered the world. The coin became successfully established in every corner of the globe reached by the Florentine merchants, and even the King of Tunisia is said to have appreciated its beauty and purity. Within a very short time the florin had achieved such a reputation on the markets that it became the base currency for exchange, rather like the dollar today. All attempts at forgery made in the hope of curbing the giddy upward spiral of Florentine power proved vain. As a saying that is still frequently used in Florence goes, 'St John will stand for no trickery' (*San Giovanni non vuole inganni*), precisely because by placing the coin between the teeth it was easy to distinguish the real gold from the harder alloy used in the forgery.

Florence became the banking centre of the world. The most successful Florentine merchants, who had become inordinately wealthy, reinvented themselves as bankers. There is no doubt at all about the fact that, at the time, many of the richest people in the world were Florentines, so much so that they were able to make loans – at very high interest rates – even to the likes of the King of France and the King of England.

It was indeed precisely one such loan, of an astronomical sum that was never repaid, that triggered the start of the city's economic downfall. Things began to turn nasty when what later became known as the 'Hundred Years' War' broke out in 1337 between England and France. The Florentine bankers Bardi and Peruzzi had for some time been the official moneylenders to the King of England, Edward III. When the king asked them to finance his military expedition against France, solemnly promising to repay the loan with all due interest, the two bankers were reluctant but could not refuse. As the war continued to swallow up vast amounts of money, the banks' customers began to be alarmed by the worsening of the crisis and rushed to withdraw their capital, which rapidly led to the bankruptcy of both companies.

The Florentine chronicler Giovanni Villani, who was also a merchant and a banker, calculated the total amount of the loan made to Edward III as 1,365,000 gold florins. It has also recently been calculated that at current value, including simple and compound interest, England's debt to Florence would be so huge that it could scarcely be equalled by the value of the entire kingdom. But the English can sleep easy: there's no risk of England being sold at auction to repay the debt to Florence! Indeed, according to the customs of the time, it was believed that the souls of insolvent debtors were condemned to hell for eternity, and such was the fate reserved not only for Edward III himself, but also for the soul of his son and those of the barons, bishops and archbishops who had been jointly liable with him in his solemn commitment to Florence.

However, the idea of so many souls condemned to hell weighed heavily on Gualtieri de' Bardi, heir to the family banking company, and hence also to the debt owed by the English crown. Indeed, in 1391 he decided to absolve all these noble souls who, not out of ill will but due simply to 'vicissitudes of the temporal things of this world', had been unable to repay their debt. This letter of absolution was discovered in archives in London by the Florentine scholar Armando Sapori. In it, like a good Christian, Gualtieri de' Bardi declared all the debts of the king and his dignitaries to be settled so that their souls, unless burdened by other and different sins, would be free to enter Heaven.

Another thing that Florence is famous for all over the world is the sharp wit of the Florentines – especially the artists – and the history of the city is packed with curious and funny stories that rarely appear in art history books or tourist guides. This wit, which may have been a legacy of the Etruscans, is shared to a greater or lesser degree by all the people of Tuscany. This means they have a particular gift for ironic repartee even in the most tragic circumstances. For instance, on the morning of 5 November 1966, the day after the terrible flood struck

Fig. 1 - Enlarged reproduction of the obverse and reverse of the Florin, the coinage of the ancient Florentine Republic

Florence, when everyone in the city was trying desperately to salvage what could be saved from the houses and shops devastated by water and mud, pasted onto the caved-in shutter of a shop with its entire contents destroyed was a notice saying: 'Closed, because today the owner is somewhat irritable'.

The tourists who visit Florence and admire the numerous works of art would observe them with even greater interest if they knew the many curious facts and the frequently comical episodes that are hidden beneath the solemnity and magnificence of these masterpieces. And how many interesting and quirky stories about these same masterpieces could the artists who created them tell the tourists if they were still alive? For instance, why did Michelangelo sculpt the statue of *David*? And what happened when he finished it? How many visitors know the answers to these and so many other questions about the famous artworks of Florence?

This is why the author, a died-in-the-wool Florentine who deeply loves his city and has over the years become well-informed about the 'hidden' historic and artistic events that have taken place in Florence, has decided to share the results of his research in this little book, which I sincerely hope will make for easy and entertaining reading.

The Secrets of Florence consists of lots of amusing stories, anecdotes, interesting facts and events, and intriguing curiosities. Some of these episodes really took place and are historically documented, while others are more legendary and have been handed down by popular tradition. They offer the reader a 'behind the scenes' view of the artistic reality of Florence that few people are familiar with.

THE ORIGINS OF FLORENCE

Florence had its origins in an Etruscan settlement derived from Fiesole (the ancient *Faesulae*), the city that still overlooks Florence from its hill above. The foundation dates to around 150 BC, probably built over the remains of a Villanovan settlement. Its first inhabitants were Etruscans, in addition to travellers and merchants – mostly Roman – passing through along the banks of the Arno. It is rather curious to note that, despite having been founded by the Etruscans, neither the political structure nor the name of this city were typically Etruscan. Unlike Fiesole, which was governed by a *lucumo* (or *lauchme*) and had an Etruscan name, the newly-founded city had a typically Latin name, *Florentia* (more on this in the next chapter), and also a different type of government based on a kingdom, albeit a small one. But the small kingdom didn't last long: only 90 years. The era of Rome governed by Etruscan kings was long past, and *Florentia* shared the fate of the entire Etruscan League which inevitably had to come to terms with Rome, after having consistently refused to submit to its dominion. In the end, Rome could not consider this attitude as anything less than rebellion, and the Roman senate sent its best legions under the command of Lucius Portius Cato against *Faesulae* and the little kingdom of *Florentia* which, at the time, had a king whose name could not have been better suited. He was in fact called Fiorino, although sadly he did not enjoy the same success as the future coin of the same name.

Faesulae, in the safety of a well-defended hilltop fortress, succeeded in avoiding destruction, whereas *Florentia*, built in the plain on the north bank of the Arno with few walls and a small army, was unable to escape the fury of the Roman legionaries. It was razed to the ground as an example to all the other rebel cities, erasing every trace of walls and buildings down to their foundations. King Fiorino died at the head of his soldiers, thus being saved from the fate of seeing the ploughshares pass over the ruins of his *Florentia*, which was literally wiped off the face of the earth. Where there had been walls, mansions and houses there would now be cultivated fields. The lands on which the city had stood were sold at auction or assigned to the veterans of the Roman dictator Sulla.

However, since these veterans were used to fighting wars and hankering after the fleshpots of Rome rather than to ploughing fields and growing crops, they soon came to an agreement with the Etruscan inhabitants of *Faesulae* to rebuild a new city with houses and marble mansions, a forum, an amphitheatre and so on: in a word all the luxuries they were accustomed to and could not do without. Catiline – who had taken refuge in *Faesulae* after his rebellion against Rome – lent his support to the construction of the new city, again named *Florentia*, which was built in 59 BC once again on the same north bank of the Arno, just a few hundred metres downstream from the earlier city. But Rome kept a strict eye on things and, when it discovered that the city had been rebuilt, it once again sent in its legions. *Faesulae* and *Florentia* strove to resist, and this time the rebel Catiline also had the support of a courageous former officer of Sulla's, Gaius Manlius.

In an epic battle fought close to Pistoia, a cobbled-together rebel army made up of Etruscan soldiers from *Faesulae* and ex-Roman legionaries who were now the new citizens of *Florentia*, under the command of Cataline and Manlius clashed with the overwhelming forces of the Roman legions commanded by Marcus Petreius. The result was a bloodbath in which Catiline and Manlius, all the other Etruscan-Florentine commanders and 3,000 brave soldiers died fighting heroically. The destructive fury of the victorious Roman legions was about to strike *Florentia* again, when word came that the Roman Senate, full of admiration for how the courageous 'rebels' had fought and fallen in the field, decreed that the city should not be destroyed again.

The small city of *Florentia* was constructed following the strict rules of the Roman castrum. It extended only for a few hundred metres in length and width (approximately 480 x 420 metres) and was crossed by two main streets that intersected in the centre at the point where you can still see, in Piazza della Repubblica, an isolated column with a figure of the nymph of plenty (*Colonna dell'Abbondanza*). These two roads, representing the *cardo maximus* and *decumanus maximus*, still exist today, although their appearance has changed. The route of the decumanus corresponds to Via degli Strozzi, Via degli Speziali and Via del Corso, and that of the cardo to Via Roma and Via Calimala. The entire city, marked by the continuous perimeter line on the enclosed map, was approximately comprised between the following present-day streets and squares: Via de' Tornabuoni, Piazza Antinori, Via de' Cerretani, Piazza del Duomo, Via del Proconsolo, Piazza San Firenze, Piazza della Signoria, and Via delle Terme.

The forum, which was the commercial centre of city life, was where Piazza della Repubblica is now, close to the point where the ancient Florentines placed the column mentioned above with the nymph of plenty as a good augury of prosperity and wealth, as well as marking the geometrical centre of the city. The column that can be seen today is not the original

Roman one, which was corroded and ravaged by time. But since the Florentines never wanted to be without this particular good luck charm of theirs, every time that the column became worn or crumbled, they always erected another one in the same place. In more recent times the precise location was shifted by a few metres for reasons of traffic circulation.

Within a short time, *Florentia* began to boast many buildings emulating the opulence of Rome. The Campidoglio

Fig. 2 - The pillar near the Baptistery of San Giovanni commemorating the miracle of the dead tree restored to life

was constructed, that is a temple dedicated to the Capitoline Triad – Jupiter, Juno, and Minerva – the three most important divinities of the Roman world. The forum was paved with precious marble and was reached by a broad flight of steps, also in marble. Beneath it was the 'treasury' where the wealth of the state was accumulated and stored along with the most valuable ex-votos.

Florentia also had its own theatre which could hold no less than 10,000 spectators. The slope of what is now Via de' Gondi, which descends from Piazza della Signoria towards Piazza San Firenze along the side of Palazzo Vecchio, corresponds to the tiers of seats of the ancient theatre. The city had around 25,000 inhabitants at the time, and by Roman standards such a large number of citizens called for several bathing establishments. One of these was close to what is now Via delle Terme (close to the Palazzo di Parte Guelfa), while another large baths complex was under street level in what is now Piazza della Signoria, as recent excavations in the piazza have shown.

In the imperial era *Florentia* was a fully-fledged Roman *municipium* and, like every municipium worthy of its name, it could not be without its own aqueduct. This impressive infrastructure was duly constructed to carry the water from the Val Marina spring on Monte Morello, channelling it on the back of the characteristic catenary arches through Rifredi, along what is now Via Vittorio Emanuele right into the centre of the city. Here it flowed into the large distribution cistern, known as the *caput acquae*. This was close to what is now Via di Capaccio, the name deriving from the original Latin term.

And, to cap it all, *Florentia* also had an amphitheatre! *Faesulae* too had a theatre, but not an amphitheatre, and the Florentine amphitheatre was one of the largest of the time, with a seating capacity of 20,000. The citizens, as well as people from *Faesulae* and elsewhere, were able to enjoy performances well worthy of Rome, with gladiator fights, wild animals, and lots of gore! Just to give you an idea of how important Florence was at the time, this amphitheatre was the fifth largest in the entire Roman Empire, with a perimeter of 335 metres and the diameters of its ellipses measuring 113 and 64 metres. The only larger amphitheatres were those of Rome, Pompeii, Verona, and Pozzuoli.

Fig. 3 - The characteristic Florentine lion known
as the 'Marzocco' (by Donatello)

There is an interesting anecdote that shows how *Florentia* knew how to command respect. Since Rome was subject to the frequent flooding of the Tiber, the imperial court had the idea of rerouting some of its more important tributaries towards the Arno. *Florentia*, being quite rightly alarmed – since it frequently suffered floods itself from its own river – objected and immediately sent a delegation that was duly received by the emperor, whose name is not mentioned. Nor is it known exactly what arguments were advanced by the Florentine ambassadors, but they were evidently highly effective since the outcome was that the emperor gave up the idea and it was never raised again!

I should like to end these notes on Roman Florence by mentioning a very important temple that was dedicated to the god Mars. It was demolished when Florence ceased to be pagan, but originally stood just a stone's throw from where the beautiful Baptistery of San Giovanni stands now. As time passed, Florence was gradually converted to Christianity, significantly influenced by the martyrdom of saints such as San Miniato and Santa Reparata during the persecutions of imperial Rome. However, despite their conversion to the Christian faith, the Florentines continued to be superstitious. Although they knew they had no choice but to demolish the pagan temple of Mars – the god of war who had been their protector up to then – they drew the line at demolishing the equestrian statue of the god that was inside the temple. You never know, they reasoned, he might even have been stirred to revenge, so that it was safer not to push their luck. Therefore, instead of destroying the statue, which was carved in stone, they moved it to a wooden bridge over the Arno that stood exactly where what remains of the first and most famous bridge in Florence – the Ponte Vecchio – still stands today. This made the Florentines feel that they had rightly hedged their bets. They had

Fig. 4 - Another of the many lions that symbolised
the strength and power of Florence

duly elected St John the Baptist as their new patron, but had
not totally reneged their former protector. In other words, it
was considered expedient 'not to take unnecessary risks!'

The definitive triumph of Christianity in Florence took
place in 403 with the appointment as bishop of Zenobius, who
was later canonised. The story is told in Florence that after
the death of Zenobius, while his body was being transported
towards what was then the church of Santa Reparata (where the
cathedral of Florence now stands), the coffin bearing his body
brushed against a dead elm tree which immediately returned to
life sprouting a multitude of tender green leaves. Is this truth
or legend? One thing is certain: since time immemorial a pillar
bearing a cross has stood on the north side of the Baptistery
of San Giovanni to commemorate the miracle, which had an

undeniable symbolic value. Sanctity brought new life to that ancient 'Roman camp' that had become arid and barren of civic virtue; Christianity brought new life to a spiritually reawakened populace amidst the ruins of the Roman civilisation.

After this, Florence suffered many tribulations at the hands of the barbarian hordes of Radagaisus (in 405), the barbarians of Theodoric and, during the clash between the Goths and the Byzantines, the siege of Totila's Ostrogoths in 537. These were probably the darkest times that the city of Florence had to live through, so much so that it is said that in such periods of hardship the populace was forced by hunger and despair to eat the grass growing in the fields.

Things improved somewhat in Florence under the Lombards (from 570). The first convents for nuns began to be built and large religious estates were created. However, the twilight period was not yet over and was to continue for several centuries, albeit without returning to the dire conditions just described. After this last time of suffering, finally Florence slowly began to grow in importance once again, and by the year 1000 had already returned to a position of prominence, even though it was not yet politically independent.

1250 was a very important date that marked the authentic rebirth of Florence with its own political structure known as the *primo popolo*. This date is also important because it marked the advent of the first example of a democratic constitution in the whole of the Western world. The symbol of the city, which had previously been a white lily on a red field, was transformed into a red lily on a white field. In the same period another emblem of the city's strength, and its independence from the German Emperor to which it had hitherto been subject, emerged in the form of the *Marzocco*, the characteristic Florentine seated lion with one paw resting on the heraldic shield bearing the lily. Why was the lion chosen as the symbol of independence? Because the symbol of oppression was the German imperial eagle, and the lion was the heraldic adversary of the eagle. The entire struggle between the Guelphs (supporters of the Pope and of civic independence) and the Ghibellines (supporters of the emperor) was symbolically represented either by a lion tearing an eagle to pieces or by an eagle clawing a lion. So, there was nothing strange about the Florentine *primo popolo* choosing the lion as their emblem, and lions carved in stone are to be seen scattered all over the historic centre of the city. Since at this time the authority of the *podestà* tended to be of Ghibelline inclination, to give greater strength to its own *capitano*, the Guelph *popolo* organised the citizens into 20 military units, each of which had its own standard bearing strange symbols including a preponderance of lions.

Since even all these painted and sculpted lions were not enough, the Florentine *popolo* also wanted a real, live lion, which was kept closed in a cage in Piazza San Giovanni. However, one day the lion keepers failed to shut the cage properly and the lion escaped. The whole city was gripped by fear, especially when the lion took into its jaws a little boy who had managed to break free from his mother. Although we know that the name of this boy was Orlando, the accounts of the episode are not all exactly in agreement. The dominant version is that the lion probably didn't actually take the child into its jaws, but rather caught his shirt between its teeth and carried him along dangling from its mouth in the way animals normally carry their young. It seems that the lion carried the boy for a good stretch, from Piazza San Giovanni, where the cage was, as far as Orsanmichele (in what is now Via dei Calzaiuoli), and that when it arrived there it entered the chapel that already existed at the time. At this point the child's mother, whom the crowd had been trying to hold back, managed to break through and ran into the church where she confronted the lion and literally ripped her son from its mouth. Everyone was astonished, and when they realised that the little Orlando had not a single scratch and saw how the lion let itself be taken back calmly and quietly to its cage, many began to speak of a miracle.

From then on there were two lions, a male and a female, to avoid the risk that if the single lion were to die they would be left without lions, which might have negative repercussions on the prosperity of the city. Having two lions allowed the Florentines to sleep easy, and they were extremely proud of this very special menagerie. One day, the lioness gave birth to two cubs – something that was truly exceptional for lions in captivity – and, amidst general rejoicing, this event was interpreted as the best possible augury of the glorious destiny that fate had in store for Florence.

Fig. 5 - A comparison between the iris pallida (sweet iris)
and the lily of Florence clearly illustrates that the inspiration
for the Florentine symbol is drawn from this flower

HOW FLORENCE GOT ITS NAME

It would seem quite logical to attribute the name of Florence – the ancient *Florentia* – to a flower, all the more so because the symbol of the city is indeed a flower: the lily of Florence. However, reliable sources provided by authoritative scholars such as Robert Davidsohn prove that this is not the case, and that the name of Florence does not derive from a flower or a flower-covered meadow. We don't know at what time the ancient Florentines adopted the lily as the symbol of their city, but it is certain that this took place long after the foundation of the city that had been named *Florentia* from the very start. So, the lily – which, as already mentioned, was for centuries white on a red field – was created after the name of the city, erroneously interpreting the name *Florentia* as 'city of flowers'.

Moreover, it also comes naturally to wonder why the Etruscans from *Faesulae* that founded the very first city on the site gave it the strictly Latin name of *Florentia*. Wouldn't it have been more logical for the founders to give it a name of Etruscan etymology? The explanation is that the Etruscans from *Faesulae* built this new city as a riverside centre crucial to their trade, with a port on the banks of the Arno. Moreover, they had at length been accustomed to hear the travellers passing through, many of them Romans, referring to this lush plain as *florentes*, or fertile.

Therefore, despite the numerous different explanations and legends, it would certainly seem that the name of Florence, or rather *Florentia*, derives not from a flower or a flowery meadow, but rather from the fertile plain on which it was built.

THE CHURCH
OF THE BADIA FIORENTINA

The Badia Fiorentina is one of the oldest churches in Florence. It was commissioned by Willa – the widow of Uberto, Margrave of Tuscia – who wished to establish an abbey for monks dedicated to Our Lady, and work started on its construction in 978. Countess Willa was a very pious and virtuous woman and was greatly loved by the people of Florence at the time, although they were even fonder of her son, Count Ugo of Brandenburg, who was the imperial vicar, even though the Florentines preferred to call him the 'great baron'. A marble plaque visible on the outer wall of the Badia Fiorentina in Via del Proconsolo, almost opposite the Bargello, bears the following lines by Dante Alighieri:

> *Each one that bears the noble coat of arms*
> *of the great baron whose name and worth*
> *are commemorated on the feast of Thomas*

These lines from the Divine Comedy (*Paradise* XVI, 127-9) refer to the 'great baron' Ugo, who is possibly the only figure who has received – and continues to receive – from the Florentines a concrete demonstration of immense gratitude and undying recollection. Count Ugo in fact died on 21 Decem-

Fig. 6 - The church of the Badia Fiorentina

ber in the year 1001. At the time, this day was celebrated as the feast of St Thomas – even though he now appears to have been ousted by other saints – and since then, every year on 21 December a special office for the dead is celebrated in the church of the Badia as intercession for the soul of Count Ugo, Margrave of Tuscany. It seems scarcely credible, but this has taken place for over 1,000 years, as confirmed by the brothers and sisters of the Monastic Fraternities of Jerusalem, to which the church has been granted. It should also be said, as indeed

I have been able to see for myself, that this is anything but a purely formal ritual held to comply with a tradition. It is on the contrary a deeply-felt ceremony involving the entire monastic community as well as large numbers of the faithful, at which the banner of Florence is also present along with attendants in sixteenth-century costume.

The ceremony takes place in several stages. First there are the vespers, with various parts sung alternately by the choir of friars and by the nuns' sopranos, very similar to Gregorian chant. After this the mass is celebrated, again with some sung parts, in the course of which there are some very beautiful and intensely moving moments, some of them emphasised by the sound of the clarions – the old trumpets of the sixteenth-century heralds. When the mass is finished, everyone – monks, nuns, and the faithful – move towards the beautiful sarcophagus by Mino da Fiesole which contains the remains of the 'great baron', at the foot of which his iron armour is placed for the occasion. At this point, the monk celebrating the office reads a special prayer, after which he blesses the remains, and this conclusive moment too is accompanied by the sound of the trumpets of the attendants and standard-bearers of the banner of Florence.

It should also be noted that the coat of arms of the noble baron was striped, with vertical bands in white and red. The fact that these were the same colours as the symbol of the city, which at the time was a white lily on a red field, was seen as yet another connection between the wise ruler and the people of Florence. But this was certainly not the reason why Count Ugo was so much loved by both the citizens and those who lived in the country. His greatest merit was the wisdom he displayed in performing his imperial mandate, which allowed him to make Florence into the most important city of Tuscia, or Tuscany. He was a truly wise and good man, and he governed the city

Fig. 7 - The tomb of the 'great baron' Count Ugo, Margrave of Tuscany

at length with scrupulous honesty and great skill and sense of justice. These gifts were very rare in a powerful lord who could have exerted his authority as imperial bishop in quite a different manner, and it was this that aroused the people's feelings of gratitude and even affection.

It is said that Ugo was in the habit of travelling incognito through the country, stopping to chat with the labourers in the fields and with the craftsmen in the villages, speaking ill of himself, that is accusing the Margrave of mismanagement and lack of provision and assistance. This was his way of finding out what the people thought about him. It seems incredible, but the people would turn angrily upon this slanderous stranger, defending and praising their ruler and expressing their extreme gratitude. Apropos this, we have to bear in mind that there is no certain documentation of these events, which have been handed down by the stories of the monks. Nevertheless, we have reason to consider them reliable, since if after over a thousand years the 'great baron' is still honoured and remembered possibly more than any other man on earth, then evidently there must be some truth in such stories.

Count Ugo, Margrave of Tuscany, died in Pistoia, and since he was greatly loved throughout his realm, the Florentines were afraid that the citizens of Pistoia would wish to bury him in one of their churches. To prevent this, they resorted to a stratagem, saying that the margrave was merely seriously ill and wished to return to Florence. They duly set his corpse upon a horse with a servant in the saddle who held him upright beneath the armpits, and in this way brought him back to Florence to be buried with all due pomp in the church of the Badia Fiorentina. This church underwent various alterations over time, most recently in the seventeenth century, but Ugo's tomb was never moved and can still be admired today inside the church in the magnificent sarcophagus already mentioned, sculpted by Mino da Fiesole, one of the greatest sculptors of the fifteenth century.

Special thanks are due to the Monastic Fraternities of Jerusalem for their kind assistance and the permission to take and publish the photograph of the interior of the church.

Fig. 8 - The Gate of Paradise with the porphyry
columns donated by the Pisans

THE SMOKED COLUMNS OF THE BAPTISTERY OF SAN GIOVANNI

Florence is a city with a wealth of stories, but it's not always easy to know whether to classify them as truth or legend. Sometimes they don't have sufficient historic documentation to qualify as real facts. On the other hand, it's also hard to see them merely as legends since artistic and monumental evidence of them does exist, visible to everyone, so that the substantial reality of the facts related cannot be entirely ruled out.

Given such doubts, all we can do is take a closer look at some of these tangible and curious testimonies that can only be explained by taking as good, albeit with reservations, the accounts of popular tradition, as in the case of the strange columns set at either side of the door of the Baptistery of San Giovanni.

Looking at the Baptistery with one's back to the cathedral, we can admire the splendid bronze door known as the 'Gate of Paradise', a fifteenth-century work by one of the most illustrious and famous Florentine sculptors of the time. The beauty of this door was such that when the great Michelangelo saw it, he declared it to be 'so beautiful that it is truly worthy to be the gates of Paradise', which is why it has been called by this name ever since. Lorenzo Ghiberti, who created it, was himself so pleased with it that he decided to leave to posterity, along with his normal signature in engraved letters, another one in the form of the self-portraits of himself and his son, who assisted him, visible in high relief among the decorative medallions surrounding the panels.

At the sides of this door, at a slight distance from it, are two ancient porphyry columns, which perhaps few people notice, believing them to be an integral part of the architecture of the Baptistery. These two columns, which on closer observation can be seen to have traces of an ancient exposure to the smoke of a fire, are instead war booty, even though they were not looted by the Florentine army but given to the city by the Pisans in gratitude after the war of the Balearic Islands fought in 1115. Therefore, these two columns have nothing to do with the Romanesque architecture of the Baptistery. So how did they come to be there? The only answer is to be found in popular tradition, since no other source mentions these columns, despite the fact that they have been in that same place, visible and tangible, since time immemorial. So, all we can do is to tell this curious story, with the clarification that the context of the events that gave rise to this story is based on rigorously documented historic episodes that really took place.

In the Middle Ages Florence and Pisa were constant rivals, essentially for reasons of a commercial nature and of political importance. They were often at war with each other and lost no opportunity for reciprocal attack and offence even in times of peace. As one old Florentine saying goes 'It's better to have a death in the house that to have a Pisan at the door', although the Pisans actually claim that this was their proverb, and that it originally ran 'It's better to have a death in the house than a Florentine at the door'. So who actually said it first, a Florentine or a Pisan? We shall never know.

But those really were very strange times. It could even happen that the proudest and most unbending enemies could

32

get to the point of shaking hands in all sincerity if certain political or commercial circumstances made it expedient. And so it happened that, at the beginning of the twelfth century the continual raids of Saracen pirates rendered commercial river traffic along the Arno very unsafe, to the detriment of both Florence and Pisa. Something had to be done quickly to prevent the ruin of the two cities, whose fortunes were based primarily on trade. Pisa had a great port on the sea at the mouth of the Arno and, unlike Florence, possessed a great fleet of ships. Therefore, of the two cities united against the Saracen threat, Pisa was better equipped to hunt down and eliminate the pirates. But Pisa could not send its fleet and its army out to sea and leave the city undefended and exposed to the attacks of the Florentines, who could have taken advantage of the situation – which was not uncommon at the time – and also exposed to the equally dreaded and similarly fierce and dangerous Lucca, which posed the most serious threat to Pisa in this period.

Pisa therefore sent an embassy to Florence to request a truce, explaining the necessity in their common interest to get rid of the Saracen pirates once and for all. Florence, seeing that this would protect its interests too, and without running any risk, willingly agreed to grant the requested truce 'on its honour'. Seeing that the Florentines were well-disposed, the Pisans decided to push for more, asking that Florence should send its army to protect their city against all possible threats. Once again, the Florentines swore 'on their honour' that no one would be able to do the slightest damage to the city of Pisa in the absence of its army.

Nowadays we might think that entrusting one's undefended city to the protection of such diehard enemies as the Florentines was extremely rash and dangerous. But we have to consider that in those times there was an extraordinarily strong sense of honour in both military and civil circuits. A word of

Fig. 9 - Detail of the Gate of Paradise with the self-portraits in high relief of Lorenzo Ghiberti and his son, authors of the work

honour was considered 'sacred' so that a doubt of such a kind would never have crossed the minds of the Pisans.

And so, in 1113 the Pisans set off with their army and their fleet to hunt down the terrible pirates while, true to its word, the Florentine army set up camp two miles outside Pisa to guard and protect the city. The commander preferred not to actually enter the city for fear that some foot soldier or knight might bother the Pisan women, which would have been a terrible slur on Florentine honour, or that the soldiers might cause harm of any kind to the people of Pisa. Indeed, he even issued an order that no Florentine should dare to enter the city without a specific order. However, it happened that a young Florentine knight, who was in love with a Pisan girl, disobeyed the commander's order and succeeded in entering

34

the city by night. When he left the city to return to the camp he was seen and immediately captured by the Florentine sentinels on guard. When he was brought before the commander, he was not even tried but immediately sentenced to death by hanging. This sad story greatly moved the people of Pisa, and several Pisan nobles visited the Florentine commander to beg remission of the sentence for the poor young man. But the commander was inflexible, even though by then the entire city of Pisa was against him and in favour of the young lover. The emotional involvement of the Pisans was by then out of control because, when all was said and done, the young knight had done nothing wrong.

As the day of the hanging drew close, and in view of the obstinate determination of the Florentine commander, in a last desperate attempt to save the young man, the Pisans informed the commander that they would never permit this unjust capital punishment on Pisan land. At this point they were convinced that they had achieved their objective, but sadly they had underestimated the famous shrewdness of the Florentines. In fact, the overly severe but artful Florentine commander immediately concocted a crafty plan to carry out the sentence despite the Pisan veto. So, the Pisans didn't want the execution to take place on Pisan soil? Very well! The commander summoned one of his officers and ordered him to buy a tiny plot of land, just large enough to set up the gallows: that land was Florentine to all effects and purposes, and it was thus that the young knight was hanged.

The Pisans' hunting down of the Saracen pirates was a complete success: their ships were destroyed and their base on the island of Majorca was also conquered and sacked. The Pisan fleet returned home with a fine array of spoils of war, including the very porphyry columns that we talked about at the beginning of this chapter. It was said that these pillars

Fig. 10 - The Baptistery of San Giovanni

were magic, an art in which the Saracens were considered to be expert. It seems that all you had to do was to stand behind one of these columns to be able to see – through the reflected images of the people who passed close by – whether they were thieves, forgers, murderers or traitors. So, in order to thank the Florentines for the absolute honesty and correctness with which they had guarded their city, the Pisans decided to offer these two columns as a gift, which they duly presented strangely wrapped up in large pieces of heavy red cloth.

No sooner was the truce ended than the suspicion and badmouthing between the Pisans and Florentines immediately resumed, in actual fact even before the Florentine army had returned home. Why on earth were these 'magical' columns wrapped up in red cloth? The suspicious Florentines removed the cloths to find that the columns had been exposed to the smoke of a fire, which immediately convinced them of the treachery of the Pisans. The fact is that since the pillars were war booty from a Saracen base on the island of Majorca that had been sacked and very plausibly set fire to, the smoke that blackened them was fairly easy to explain. But the Florentines preferred to believe that they had been deliberately torched by the Pisans to remove all their magic power, so that it would be impossible to discover just how much the Pisans were thieves, forgers, murderers and traitors! And so, Florence placed these columns at the sides of the door of the Baptistery, presumably to remind posterity of the honesty of the Florentines and the deceit of the Pisans.

A few details about the Baptistery

The Baptistery is one of the finest examples of pure Romanesque art. It was begun in the second half of the eleventh century, erected close to the site of a previous Roman temple dedicated to Mars. One of the doors is by Andrea Pisano, while the other two are by Lorenzo Ghiberti. In the interior are mosaics attributed to Coppo di Marcovaldo and Cimabue. The construction was completed in 1225 by the Franciscan friars, who also adorned the front of the scarsella with coloured glass mosaics, while the beautiful green and white marble decoration of the exterior was executed later by Arnolfo di Cambio in 1294.

Fig. 11 - The dome of the cathedral of Florence (Santa Maria del Fiore)

THE CATHEDRAL OF FLORENCE
(SANTA MARIA DEL FIORE)

The cathedral of Florence was built over the remains of the pre-existing early Christian church dedicated to Santa Reparata. Construction began in 1296 in pure Tuscan Gothic style to a design by the great Florentine architect Arnolfo di Cambio. Arnolfo was even granted tax exemption because he was working on the greatest Christian monument of that time. The cathedral of Florence is indeed of impressive size: 153 metres long, a width ranging from 38 to 90 metres, 55 metres high in the nave, height of the dome 88 metres, along with a lantern of a further 20 metres. However, since Arnolfo died in 1300, he worked on it for only four years.

The cathedral was designed to demonstrate to the world the position of absolute political and commercial supremacy held by Florence and, in substance, the power and greatness of the city. However, the construction of this marvel had exorbitant costs; it took no less than 140 years to build and literally cost the earth! Although the tax revenues of Florence were very high, there was never enough money. We have already mentioned several times the craftiness of the Florentines who have somehow always managed to get out of a sticky situation through ingenious and sometimes even inspired solutions. So, what could the city authorities do to scrape together more money for the construction of the magnificent cathedral? The

Fig. 12 - Overall view of the cathedral

answer they came up with was simply brilliant: they would charge a fine to anyone heard to blaspheme.

And so, the hunt for the blasphemers began, and in effect a great many were discovered, especially among the artisans and even the very labourers who were working on the construction of Santa Maria del Fiore. The proceeds of these fines would be used to pay for the worked stone for the huge building. This brainwave provided a brilliant solution to the problem of assuring significant new funding for the cathedral worksite, which was now proceeding under the direction of Francesco Talenti, who had taken over from Arnolfo di Cambio.

When the magnificent construction got to the level of the dome, the problems that arose were much more serious than those easily resolved with a tax on swearing. No architect had ever built a dome of this size. The structural problems were such that, if a safe construction method were not found, there was a risk that the immense dome would collapse under its own weight during the building. It was decided to announce a public competition, and numerous projects and designs were submitted: some were too daring and risky, others were feasible but too expensive, and yet others were incredibly absurd. Among this latter group it is interesting to mention one in particular, which greatly amused the judges of the competition. One of the entrants proposed building a huge dome made of earth, a sort of oval mountain with numerous gold florins mixed in with the earth. This species of 'formwork' of earth was to be the support for the bricks of the actual construction which, sustained by the earthwork, would not risk collapsing. Once the construction was complete and in place, the earth could then be removed in the certainty that the dome could no longer collapse. And how would all that earth be removed from inside the dome? No problem at all! The citizens would all be invited to come along, armed with their wagons, carts, wheelbarrows, spades and shovels etc. to carry off the earth with the florins that were hidden in it, and those who found them in the earth they were carrying off would be allowed to keep them. Naturally, this project was not selected, and the competition was won by Filippo Brunelleschi's proposal which, although daring, proved in the end to be the most convincing. Brunelleschi (Filippo di ser Brunellesco) had come up with an ingenious solution for a self-supporting structure, a dome built with two concentric shells, and by adopting this system the dome would support itself during construction without the risk of collapse.

Fig. 13 - View of the dome of the cathedral clearly showing the 'gallery' by Baccio d'Agnolo which was begun but never completed

COLUMBUS'S EGG OR BRUNELLESCHI'S EGG?

One should not think that Filippo Brunelleschi won the competition for the dome hands down. On the contrary, initially the representatives of the Opera del Duomo – the institution set up to supervise the construction of the cathedral – and those of the Arte della Lana (the Wool Guild) were anything but convinced of the validity of his project. Indeed, when Brunelleschi claimed he would be able to construct the dome without the use of wooden scaffolding, he was taken for mad and asked to leave the room where the committee was gathered. But Brunelleschi pretended not to have heard and continued to speak, producing knowledgeable but far from convincing arguments to support his design. After having been asked to leave several times to no avail, the committee eventually had him taken away forcibly by the ushers who carried him bodily from the room.

Tradition attributes to Brunelleschi the expedient known to everyone as 'Columbus's egg', which consisted of making an egg stand upright simply by striking a light blow at one end on a marble table to flatten the shell very slightly and invisibly but sufficiently to ensure it did not roll over. If this extremely famous story is true, Brunelleschi's egg demonstration would have taken place at least 70 years before Christopher Columbus made a similar gesture. In attributing this episode to the great architect, it is said that Brunelleschi, irritated by not having had a fair hearing by the committee, challenged the other competing architects saying: 'whosoever could make an egg stand upright on a flat piece of marble should build the cupola, since thus each man's intellect would be discerned'.

It was certainly not on account of this episode that the committee changed its opinion about Brunelleschi's project. In actual fact, before the work was entrusted to him, he had to produce quite different and more challenging proofs to support his theory and demonstrate his capacity to construct smaller-scale, but still daring, cupolas such as that of the Barbadori chapel in the church of Santa Felicita and that of Sant'Iacopo Sopr'Arno.

The construction of Santa Maria del Fiore was completed in 1436 and it was solemnly consecrated in the same year, even though it was still missing the lantern on top of the dome and the decoration of the facade was still unfinished, and was still in rough stone like that of the Basilica di San Lorenzo even today. The lantern was completed later, again by Filippo Brunelleschi, while the current decoration of the facade, which many people believe to be authentically Gothic, was instead realised in a greatly criticised neo-Gothic style by the architect Emilio De Fabris in the nineteenth century.

CURIOUS FACTS

The ball at the top of the lantern of the dome is no longer the original made by Verrocchio, which was struck by lightning on 17 January 1600 and fell into the square below where it shattered into fragments. The current ball, reconstructed in 1602, is larger than the previous one and it is said it could easily hold within a dining table and chairs for eight people!

But there is another even more curious fact about the dome. Looking at it from the outside you can see that the brickwork on the upper part of the drum that the dome rests on is still unfinished. This work was begun in the form of an arched balcony, but only the section facing towards Via dell'Oriuolo and Via del Proconsolo was finished, leaving the rest uncovered. Why was it never finished? A famous anecdote provides the answer. The balcony was begun in 1506 by Baccio d'Agnolo, who worked on it up to 1515 when he heard of the critical comment made on it by the great Michelangelo, who declared that it reminded him of a cricket's cage! This criticism so discouraged poor Baccio that he stopped working on the balcony and neither he nor anyone else ever resumed it.

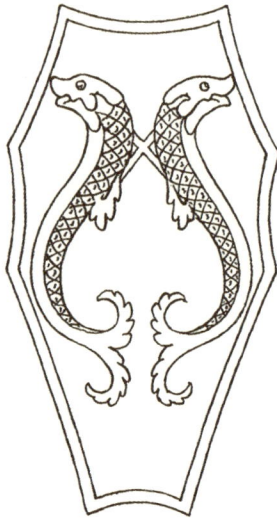

Fig. 14 - Heraldic crest of the Pazzi family

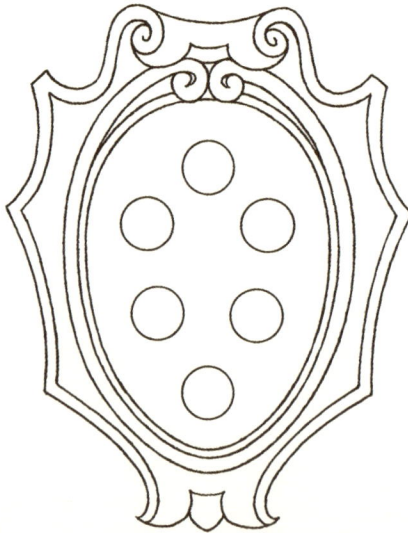

Fig. 15 - Heraldic crest of the Medici family

A BLOODY EPISODE

Five centuries ago, a bloody episode took place in the cathedral of Florence that has gone down in history under the name of the 'Pazzi Conspiracy', in the course of which the brother of Lorenzo the Magnificent, the young Giuliano de' Medici, lost his life.

The Medici lords of Florence were greatly loved by the people, at least in that period, but they were hated by several of the oldest and most powerful Florentine families, including the noble Pazzi dynasty. Another powerful enemy of the Medici was Pope Sixtus IV who, far from being a 'Holy Father', was a nepotist pope who was much more concerned with earthly rather than spiritual interests, and was supported in his aspirations by Francesco Salviati, Archbishop of Pisa. While the Pazzi harboured their hatred, outwardly pretending to be friends of the Medici, there was a situation of extreme tension and constant reciprocal conflict between the Medici on one side and the pope and Archbishop Salviati on the other. Everything came to a head when Salviati sent Raffaele Riario to Florence to organise with the Pazzi family a plot to kill Lorenzo and Giuliano de' Medici. Raffaele Riario was little more than a lad at the time; as the pope's nephew, he had been made cardinal at the age of just eighteen and, despite his youth, his office allowed him to greatly facilitate the engineering of the plot.

A series of festivities were organised in the course of which it would have been fairly easy to kill the Medici brothers, but the plan was not carried through because Giuliano was ill and did not take part. After this plan had been foiled, it was decided to carry out the attempt in the cathedral during mass, when it was certain that both Lorenzo and Giuliano would be present.

On the morning of 26 April 1478 everything was ready and, as the bells of the cathedral rang out to announce the mass, the conspirators began to enter the cathedral with their weapons concealed in their clothes. However, at the very last moment something happened which seemed to destine the conspiracy to another failure. Lorenzo was considerably stronger than Giuliano and the man assigned to kill him, Giovan Battista da Montesecco, was an expert man-at-arms, but when he realised that he was expected to kill Lorenzo in the cathedral and, what's more, at the very moment of the consecration, he refused outright, saying that he was willing to kill, but not in church and not in a sacrilegious manner. There was no time to find a suitable replacement and so the task of killing Lorenzo was hastily taken on by the priest Stefano Bagnoni and the notary of the Apostolic Camera, Antonio da Volterra.

Meanwhile, Lorenzo and Giuliano were late in arriving and the conspirators began to fear that some other unforeseen circumstance might save the designated victims. Francesco de' Pazzi and Bernardo Bandini left the church to watch for the brothers as they left their palazzo in Via Largo – now Via Cavour – which was clearly visible from the cathedral square. When they saw Lorenzo and Giuliano emerge, they ran towards them, pretending to embrace them while they were actually checking to see whether they were wearing armour or coats of mail under their garments. The two young men were practically defenceless. Giuliano had no weapons at all, and Lorenzo only a sword. Reassured, the two conspirators smiling in friendly fashion escorted the brothers into the cathedral and as far as the altar.

The mass began. As fate would have it, close to the group of the conspirators and their chosen victims, standing among the faithful there was also the famous humanist philosopher and intellectual Agnolo Poliziano, who was a friend of the Medici, who went on to recount the details of what happened to the world. When the celebration of the mass reached the moment of the elevation of the host, the altar server rang the silver bell and the faithful all knelt, including Lorenzo and Giuliano. But the conspirators did not kneel and, while the sacred host was raised aloft, Bernardo Bandini and Francesco de' Pazzi moved towards Giuliano unsheathing their daggers. Bandini struck the first blow, stabbing him through the chest. Although Giuliano was seriously wounded, he tried to escape but fell to the ground after just a few steps, whereupon Francesco de' Pazzi immediately jumped upon him, stabbing him over and over. Meanwhile Stefano Bagnoni and Antonio da Volterra attacked Lorenzo; Antonio grabbed him by the shoulder and wounded him in the throat, although not seriously. Lorenzo jumped to his feet and drew his sword, setting his attackers to flight. Immediately, before even knowing of Giuliano's death and with the help of his friend Poliziano, he ran to take refuge in the sacristy. Later, when he heard about his brother, he returned to the palazzo in Via Largo escorted by his armed friends, and there he began implementing his ruthless revenge.

Racing round the city on horseback, the Pazzi tried in vain to rouse the Florentines against the Medici. The people loved Lorenzo and Giuliano too much, and they were also enraged against the conspirators for the sacrilegious assassination. Just one hour later Archbishop Salviati, with a rope around his neck, was cast out of the last window of the Sala dei Duecento in Palazzo Vecchio, and six of the other co-conspirators kept him macabre company dangling from the other windows, with the naked body of the young Francesco de' Pazzi among them. Only Bernardo Bandini managed to escape, taking refuge in Constantinople, no less. But even in that distant land there was great esteem for Lorenzo de' Medici and so the sultan had him arrested and sent him back in chains to Florence where, a year and a half after the plot, he too was hanged.

The pope's nephew, the young cardinal Raffaele Riario, after having been kept in prison for two weeks with the fear of feeling a rope tightened around his neck at any time, was instead freed and sent back to Rome.

In Via del Proconsolo, on the corner with Borgo degli Albizi, there is a beautiful fifteenth-century palazzo adorned on the corner by an elegant coat of arms with fluttering ribbons billowing over the two walls. This is the Pazzi family crest, on which we can see two leaping dolphins shown back to back with their tails almost touching, on a field scattered with small crosses. Closer to the Bargello, from which it was once separated by a lane, is another narrow fourteenth-century house that was the residence of the Pazzi. After the plot in which Giuliano lost his life, no one ever mentioned the name again and these houses were confiscated along with all the family's assets. Even the age-old Florentine tradition of the 'explosion of the cart' ceremony was suspended for several years to prevent any further honour being paid to the family, which enjoyed the ancestral privilege of lighting the holy fire on Easter Sunday in memory of their ancestor Pazzino dei Pazzi, a valiant veteran of the Crusades.

THE EXPLOSION OF THE CART

Anyone who happens to be in Florence on Easter Sunday will be able to witness a unique spectacle taking place in the cathedral square: the explosion of the cart. This is a very old Florentine tradition connected with a legend that is lost in the mists of time. But is it right to speak of a legend? In actual fact, the historic foundation of the story is not proven, but it is said that when Pope Urban II announced the First Crusade to liberate Jerusalem, many Florentine knights joined forces with the troops of Godfrey of Bouillon, and this much is historically documented. Legend tells – and it is far from improbable – that among these knights was an ancestor of the Florentine Pazzi family called Pazzino. Legend also tells that this same Pazzino de' Pazzi was the first crusader to scale the walls of Jerusalem and that the commander, Godfrey of Bouillon, gave him two pieces of stone taken from the Holy Sepulchre in recognition of his bravery. When Pazzino returned home, the Florentine church awarded to the valiant crusader and his descendants the privilege of lighting the holy fire on Easter Sunday with the sparks created by rubbing together the two pieces of stone, which were evidently flint, in the old Florentine cathedral of Santa Reparata.

Fig. 16 - The explosion of the cart (courtesy of FOTO LOCCHI – Florence)

Later – we don't know exactly when, but definitely hundreds of years ago – the Florentine tradition of the 'explosion of the cart' emerged, in which this same holy fire is used to light the fireworks on the cart, as it still is today.

Is the story of Pazzino de' Pazzi truth or legend? One thing is certain: for as long as there is memory of the explosion of the cart, the ceremony of the lighting of the holy fire was always entrusted to a member of the Pazzi family. Another curious detail – which can only be explained if the legendary tradition is taken as valid – is that at the top of the *brindellone*, which is what the wagon carrying the fireworks is traditionally called, there have always been four dolphins carved into the wood of the cart, and as we saw on the family crest, dolphins are the heraldic emblems of the Pazzi!

I shall leave any judgement on such things, and about whether the story is legend or truth, to the discretion of the reader and the visitor, and instead shall describe how this very old and spectacular ceremony is performed.

On the morning of Easter Sunday, accompanied by the blare of the clarions and the roll of drums of the historic football players dressed in sixteenth-century costume, a multicoloured cortege of knights and ladies, also dressed in traditional Florentine costumes, follow the standard-bearer carrying the banner of the city to Porta al Prato, where the wagon known as the *brindellone* is kept in a huge garage. The *brindellone* is an old and extremely tall ornamental wagon, polygonal in shape and ending in a pinnacle in the upper section, which has already been festooned with a huge number of fireworks over the previous days. In fact, it is not really accurate to talk about 'explosion of the cart', since the wagon itself does not explode, but rather the profusion of firecrackers, squibs, and catherine wheels in which it is covered from top to bottom.

The wagon is drawn through the streets by two large white oxen of the Chianina breed, from the part of Tuscany known as the Val di Chiana, whose heads are garlanded with flowers. The carriage is accompanied by the procession in costume and the musicians as far as the square of the cathedral where rows of seats have been installed for the numerous spectators who come to watch the spectacle, which starts with the band playing traditional music and the display of the flag-throwers. After this the Archbishop of Florence initiates the ceremony proper, which takes place in two phases: the first in the Baptistery of San Giovanni and the second in the cathedral, where the solemn Easter mass is celebrated. The holy fire is used to light the Paschal candle and the mass begins. At the moment of the Gloria, the Paschal candle is used to light a small rocket to which the *colombina* – a small dove made of papier-mâché – has been attached, which is propelled rapidly along a fine wire running between the high altar and the wagon which is standing outside the doors, between the cathedral and the baptistery. The dove makes this flight in two directions. First it flies as far as the cart, setting fire to the fuse that will set off the fireworks. Then, if all goes well – which doesn't always happen – the dove returns at the same speed back to the altar from which it set off, while the square is filled with the smoke and the deafening noise of the exploding fireworks.

Since time immemorial, although nowadays definitely less than in the past, the country folk would arrive in the city in throngs to watch the explosion of the cart. This is because it has always been a tradition to draw an augury from the flight of the dove. If all went well, that is if the dove duly set the fireworks alight and then returned to the high altar, this meant that the year's harvest would be abundant and of good quality. Otherwise, if something went amiss with the flight of the dove or the lighting of the fireworks, then this bode ill for the harvest, which might have been struck by drought or by a hailstorm that destroyed the fruit of so much hard work.

Before leaving this topic, it is interesting to look more closely at the emblematic figure of the dove. Why was a dove chosen to set alight the fireworks on the wagon? The answer seems obvious, because the dove is universally considered a symbol of peace and, effectively, it could be just that. However, when such symbolism is placed within the context of Florence, we must always take care not to take too seriously things which at first glance seem the most obvious. Indeed, there could also be another explanation, possibly more complicated but not to be underestimated since things that are too straightforward have never been a characteristic of the Florentine spirit. So, let's now take into consideration a possibly different explanation of the choice of the dove.

As already mentioned, the beautiful cathedral of Florence Santa Maria del Fiore was built over the remains of a previous early Christian church dedicated to Santa Reparata. Although it was very much smaller than the present cathedral, it was nonetheless one of the most important Christian temples and was undoubtedly the pride and glory of the Florentines who had a great veneration for the holy martyr after whom it was named. The cult of this important saint appears to have been brought to Florence by the first Christian missionaries when, in the early centuries of Christianity, Florence was still pagan. It seems very likely that Santa Reparata was actually the first church built in the city after its conversion. The remains of this ancient church were found beneath the present pavement, and can be visited via steps leading down from inside the cathedral.

There is also a legend about Santa Reparata, to which the Florentines have always given the utmost credit. Reparata was a young Eastern girl who was put to death in her native Caesarea in 250 AD during the persecution of the Roman emperor Decius. She was one of the many young Christians who suffered martyrdom because they refused to sacrifice to the pagan gods. Legend tells that when Reparata was decapitated by the executioner's sword, her soul was seen to leave her body in the shape of a dove and ascend to heaven.

Therefore, it is at least curiously coincidental that it was precisely a dove that was chosen to light the fireworks on the wagon, starting from the very heart of the cathedral built over the ruins of the ancient church dedicated to the saint whose soul was spiritually resurrected, flying towards heaven in the form of a dove.

The bridges of Florence:
The sins of the Florentines
and God's punishment

Since Roman times, the Florentines felt very strongly the need for a bridge over the Arno. The first bridge was indeed built at the beginning of the first century AD, just slightly upstream from the present Ponte Vecchio. Close to the Ponte Vecchio there still exists an ancient lane called Vicolo Marzio, running from Piazza Santo Stefano to Piazza del Pesce, which marks the exact spot where the first bridge over the Arno must have stood. In actual fact it must have been more like a wooden footbridge that only later, in 120 AD – when the Emperor Hadrian expanded the Via Cassia – began to assume the appearance of an actual bridge, much wider and supported by piers in brick masonry. The name 'Ponte Marzio' was given to it only later when, after the city was converted to Christianity, the statue of the god Mars – or assumed to be such – who had been the previous protector of the city and was now replaced by the new patron St John the Baptist, was set up at the end of the bridge. As already mentioned, the statue had been removed from the ancient temple that stood in Piazza San Giovanni and had to be demolished to make way for the 'Bel San Giovanni', the Baptistery of Florence. It is not known exactly when this bridge was moved to the point where Ponte Vecchio now stands. What we do know for certain is that it was moved and remade entirely in solid masonry in the year 972, as historically documented in the mention of a deed issued by the Bishop of Florence, Sichelmo.

Two hundred years later in October 1177, this bridge was destroyed when the Arno flooded and was rebuilt further downstream in wood while awaiting a new, permanent bridge. The replacement of the wood with masonry took about 20 years, after which Florence finally had a bridge worthy of the name, with a decent roadway of about nine metres in width paved with bricks arranged in a herringbone pattern, and no less than five masonry arches. It is strange that it appears to have been destined to house shops from the very start and, for the first time, small wooden shops overhanging the river were built along the sides of the bridge. This was the only bridge in Florence up to 1220 when requirements due to the continual expansion of the city led to the construction of a new bridge downstream, the one which – no longer original – is now named Ponte alla Carraia. At the time, this new bridge was called 'Ponte Nuovo' and, from then on, the Ponte Marzio was called 'Ponte Vecchio'.

The city was growing and its infrastructural needs with it, so that in 1227 a third bridge was built upstream of the Ponte Vecchio. It was named Ponte di Rubaconte, after a *podestà*, and later Ponte alle Grazie after a miraculous Madonna. The present bridge, rebuilt on the same spot, is also called Ponte alle Grazie. In 1252, a fourth bridge was built between the Ponte Vecchio and the Ponte Nuova, and was named after the nearby church of Santa Trinita.

In the meantime, the Ponte Vecchio itself had been considerably altered and strengthened, with towers overlooking it and crowned with battlements like a castle. Of the four bridges in existence, it certainly continued to be the most important from an urbanistic perspective, and also in architectural and economic terms. But although it was massive and fortified, the bridge was still periodically threatened by the flooding of the Arno. It was not so much the violent rush of water that battered the old masonry, but the timber that the river carried downstream during the floods. Tree trunks and beams borne along by the water crashed violently into the bridges. As long as the level of the water was not too high, the bridges with their spur-shaped piers managed to resist well, but when the water rose above the arches it was hard for the bridges to withstand the force of the water and the blows of the timbers that it carried along with such violence.

And so it happened that in the year 1333 – which later came to be known as 'the year of the great flood' – all the bridges of Florence were destroyed by the flood, swept away with a destructive fury that was possibly the most catastrophic to ever strike the city. It was at this time that the equestrian statue of Mars, which was set on a pilaster just below the Ponte Vecchio, was carried off by the raging waters never to be seen again.

The description of this apocalyptic flood left by the Florentine chronicler Giovanni Villani conveys the full tragic nature of the disaster:

In the year of Christ 1333, on the first day of November, when the city of Florence was most powerful and happy, and in a state better than she had been since the early years of the century, so it pleased God...

There follows a terrible description of the *flood of waters* that struck Florence:

For four days and four nights the sluice gates of heaven opened so that all the people lived in great fear, and all the bells of all the churches in the city pealed out continually until the waters ceased to rise; and in every house there were buckets and basins, amidst great shrieking and crying out to the merciful God for the people who were in danger, with people fleeing from their homes and from rooftop to

Fig. 17 - A view of Ponte Vecchio (detail)

rooftop, making bridges from one house to another, so that the noise
and tumult was so great that you could scarcely hear the roar of the
thunder.

The flood was seen as a divine scourge. While the astrologists sought to discover the natural causes, the theologists attributed it indubitably to a punishment from God for the sins of the Florentines. They compared it to the biblical castigation of Sodom and Gomorrah, the destruction being the price to be paid for their pride, avarice, and lust. Ultimately, it was punishment for the political and moral corruption from which Florence had drawn all its power and prosperity.

Among other things, one of the cited examples of unbridled and shameless luxury referred to the windows of the palace of the Guidi counts which were all fitted with panes of glass, a marvel and an unbelievable luxury at the time. Indeed, even the populace referred to this building with scandalised admiration as 'the crystal palace'.

But there was also another example of flagrant corruption that, according to the moralists of the time, had called down divine punishment: namely, the Florentine women guilty of taking excessive delight in fine clothing and cosmetics of every kind. In fourteenth-century Florence, women's lives were generally harsh and wretched, except for those who belonged to the higher social classes. Women spent practically their whole lives within their own four walls; if they wished to go out, they could do so only in the morning, and then only to go to mass. Once mass was over, they had to hurry home without stopping to indulge in vain gossiping along the way. For the rest of the day, they were not allowed to go out, except on rare, special occasions and events that might take place over the year, such as festivities or funerals. All the purchases for the family's needs, both for food and for other requirements, were taken care of by the men who, unlike the women, were free to go out whenever they pleased. The role of the women was to take care of all the other domestic chores: cooking, cleaning, washing, making bread, educating the children and also making all the clothes and linens. The housework was never finished and took up the entire day from dawn until late in the evening.

As mentioned, women were only allowed to go out to attend festivities in the city or other special occasions. We can easily imagine how much the women, especially young women, who spent so much time cooped up the house would look forward eagerly to those rare opportunities for diversion, joining the merrymaking crowd in dancing and singing. The women literally went crazy on such occasions, striving to set off their charms to the best, engaging in lengthy cosmetic preparations of their skin and hair, and donning their finest clothes that were nor-

Fig. 18 - The Ponte Vecchio, with the Vasari Corridor,
seen from Lungarno degli Acciaiuoli

mally kept carefully folded in the household chests. The canon
of female beauty of the time prescribed that the complexion had
to be fair. To achieve this the women would go to the greatest
lengths, washing themselves in water from the Mugnone (a river
that runs through Florence) to which they added various sub-
stances (known as *lattovari*, or electuaries, and *acquelanfe*, orange
flower water), which were actually very tough on the skin. The
number one rule was to remove every single hair from the face
and neck, even the tiniest, and this depilation was undertaken
with the greatest care, shaving the forehead, cheeks and neck with
specially-made blades of fine glass. These were authentic flaying
blades, and in addition to removing the facial hair had the added
advantage of reducing the thickness of the skin at the same time!

Another method of hair removal involved concoctions
based on quicklime, recipes for which can be found in the man-
uals of the time: 'Take well chopped and sieved quicklime and

place in an earthenware pot and boil and cook it like a poultice and then take a dram of orpiment [arsenic sulphide] and heat that too with the quicklime.' To test the efficacy of this hair-removal treatment it was recommended to 'take a hen or goose quill and dip it into the unguent, if the feathers come off it is ready; if not, it isn't.' Unfortunately, however, this depilator was so caustic that it burnt the skin as well as the hairs! And so obviously there were also recipes for unguents to use on burns: 'And if it should happen that any ulceration is caused use *populeo* [dried poplar buds] and rose oil, mixing them together, and anoint the said spot.'

But having beautiful white skin was not enough, the women also had to be blonde, in line with the French fashion and the poetry of the poets and storytellers who always sung the praises of beautiful girls with 'golden tresses'. Those who were already fair-haired tried to lighten the colour even more, while those who were dark had to resort to the 'blonding art'. This consisted of washing one's hair with *ranno* – a caustic water that was made by macerating wood or charcoal ash for many days, which was also used to wash dirty linen. Another option was to expose one's hair to the sun for days at a time, wearing a special hat known as a *solana* with a very broad brim and no crown. After the hat was put on, the hair was pulled through the open crown and then spread out evenly all over the brim so that it would be bleached by exposure to the fiery rays of the summer sun. As well as permitting the maximum spreading of the hair, the brim also served another very important purpose by preventing the sun from shining on the face, which remained in shadow and conserved its indispensable whiteness. The hair would often be further adorned with false plaits made of white and yellow silk and garlands of flowers.

As regards clothing, the more modest and demure ladies wore a full-length gown called a *socca*, clasped at the waist by a simple belt with a buckle. The *socca* had a short train behind and was slightly shorter at the front, such as to leave the hem of the petticoat in view. Over the gown, a long cloak was worn, almost always green and fastened at the front by a brooch of silvered or gilded metal. Married women would wear a white cloth over their heads, and widows a black one. While at home women wore simple cloth slippers, but when they went out they wore leather shoes with extremely high platform soles. Of course, the wealthiest ladies had gorgeous gowns of the most varied styles, made from silks, brocaded in gold and silver with lancé and boucle wefts, damasks, and samites in the most beautiful colours and often decorated with fringes, pearls, and precious stones. And so here was another reason for the divine chastisement that had literally 'rained down' on Florence.

But, to return to the bridges of Florence: the first to be rebuilt after the flood was Ponte alla Carraia, while work on the new Ponte Vecchio did not begin until 1345, to be completed in 1350. This is the very bridge that we can still admire today in all its original beauty, apart from the Vasari Corridor running above it which was added only much later. The shops on the bridge have only relatively recently come to be occupied by goldsmiths, whereas they were originally assigned to the members of the guild of butchers.

History has not passed down the name of the architect – or *capomastro*, as he was then known – responsible for building the present-day Ponte Vecchio. It may have been Neri di Fioravante, who was at the time the official *capomastro* of the Signoria, or perhaps the Dominican friar, Frà Giovanni da Campi, who had already completed the reconstruction of the Carraia bridge in 1337.

CLOSE TO SANTO STEFANO, A TRAGIC LOVE STORY THAT SEEMS LIKE A FAIRY TALE GAVE RISE TO THE GUELFS AND THE GHIBELLINES

There's a colloquial saying that many Tuscans, and especially Florentines, have been using with great frequency for many centuries, and more specifically since Easter Sunday of the year 1216. It is rare indeed, even today, that upon the accomplishment of some endeavour at least once in his or her life every Florentine has announced with satisfaction 'Cosa fatta capo ha!', which translates more or less as 'What's done is done.' However, despite the common use of this expression, even the most dyed-in-the-wool Florentines probably use it because it is familiar but are not aware of the precise meaning or where it came from.

Close to the Ponte Vecchio, between Via Por Santa Maria and Piazza del Pesce, there is another little square known as Piazza Santo Stefano al Ponte after the name of the beautiful little eleventh-century Romanesque church that overlooks it and for its closeness to the Ponte Vecchio bridge. It is a half-hidden little square that few tourists even notice, but it is well worth visiting. Who would ever think that this tiny square with its little church had such great importance in the history of Florence? And yet, it was right there, in that square and that church, that a bloody deed took place that gave rise not only to the saying mentioned above, but – even more importantly – triggered the series of feuds and vendettas that led to the emergence of the opposing parties of the Guelphs and Ghibellines. For centuries, this conflict was to influence and afflict not only the history of Florence, but also that of much of Italy, with far-reaching repercussions in the rest of Europe too.

On the other side of the Ponte Vecchio, more or less where Via Guicciardini is now, there lived a brilliant, handsome, elegant, and exceedingly rich young man called Buondelmonte de' Buondelmonti. He was what we might call a very 'eligible bachelor', and he set a lot of maidens' hearts beating faster when he left his mansion on the other side of the river and rode on horseback into the city over the Ponte Vecchio. Among the young girls who had lost their hearts to this dashing knight there were two in particular – which was of great significance in the tragic episode that ensued. One was Reparata, the daughter of Lambertuccio Amidei who, although he was neither noble nor particularly wealthy, nevertheless belonged to a leisured class that was influential in Florence at the time. The other was Beatrice, one of the two stunningly beautiful daughters of a rich widow called Aldrada Donati.

In 1216 a young friend of Buondelmonte, Mazzingo Teghini, was dubbed a knight and, as was the custom, a great banquet was organised in his honour. Occupying posts of honour among the numerous invited guests were the young Buondelmonte and a noble friend of his, Uberto degli Infangati. Many other illustrious names of the Florentine aristocracy were represented among the guests, including Lambertuccio Amidei (father of one of the girls mentioned above, in love with Buondelmonte), Oddo Arrighi (uncle of the same girl) and other nobles from the Florentine hinterland that were relatives of the Amidei and the Arrighi. These nobles belonged to the families of the Fifanti, the Uberti, the Lamberti, and the Alberti – almost all names that were to be of great importance in the history of Florence – and all had their tower-houses in the vicinity of the Ponte Vecchio and the square of Santo Stefano al Ponte.

Despite the fact that they had been invited to the same banquet, there was no love lost between the Buondelmonti and Infangati families on one side and the Amidei, Arrighi, Fifanti, Uberti, Lamberti, and Alberti on the other. However, Buondelmonte and Uberto Infangati were great friends and, as was the custom between friends at banquets, their food was served to them on a single platter. At a certain point of the festivities – undoubtedly urged on by the diners of the opposing coterie – a jester whisked away the platter piled with meat from the two friends. Buondelmonte was extremely annoyed by this disrespectful gesture, but Oddo Arrighi, an insolent knight, openly took up the defence of the boorish jester. This made Buondelmonte even angrier and also made his friend Uberto lose his temper and respond to Arrighi, challenging him with the accusation of being an outrageous liar 'Tu menti per la gola!'– literally, 'You lie in your throat!' – which was the worst insult that could be addressed to a man of honour. At this, a brawl broke out: plates and goblets were hurled and tables overturned. Buondelmonte unsheathed his sword and wounded the insolent Oddo Arrighi in the arm, effectively bringing the banquet to an end.

Obviously, the matter didn't end there. A few days later the enemies of the Buondelmonti met in the little church we mentioned, Santo Stefano al Ponte, to decide what sort of punishment should be inflicted on Buondelmonte for having wounded Oddo Arrighi. After a lively discussion, a forced marriage was decided on, which was not an uncommon way of settling feuds at the time. The bride would have to be the daughter of one of them, and the choice fell on the not beautiful, not noble, and not very rich Reparata, daughter of Lambertuccio Amidei, whom we mentioned above. For her, this was a dream come true, since she now had the unhoped-for certainty of marrying the fine knight whom she had fallen so madly in love with.

A messenger was sent to the young Buondelmonte with a parchment bearing a species of ultimatum in which he was ordered to consent to the marriage as the only way of redressing the offence. Buondelmonte was anything but a coward; however, since the anger of the banquet was now a thing of the past, he did not want to stir up any more trouble or animosity and, albeit with a heavy heart, agreed to marry the girl.

According to the customs of the time, the actual wedding – which was called *impalmamento* referring to the gesture of joining the palms in a solemn vow– was preceded by two other distinct and separate stages. The first was the *inanellamento*, the engagement in the presence of relatives, and the second was the *subarrazione*, or contract, that had to be drawn up before a notary. It was also the practice that if a man abandoned his fiancée, defaulting on his promise to marry her, he had to pay compensation to her family in the form of a fine. The fine was lower if the breach of promise took place after the engagement but before the contract, and much higher if it took place afterwards.

However, these practices were customary only as regards the ordinary people, since when engagements were broken off among the ranks of the nobility or the city aristocracy, it was usually a very different matter: the noble relatives of the rejected girl often saw the breaking off of an engagement as a very serious affront. In such cases the payment of an adequate monetary compensation was rarely deemed sufficient: more often than not the offence could be repaired only by the blood of the defaulter.

Moreover, the city authorities in a sense favoured this attitude on the part of the nobles and the magnates. The 'honour killing' in aristocratic circles fell within a rationale that was typical of the mentality of the time. Laws in this respect existed and, at least as far as they were written, did not make distinctions between rich and poor and were fairly severe. Their actual application in the context of civic life was another matter. For the ordinary people these laws were always inflexibly applied, while for the nobles and magnates there was a tendency to turn a blind eye, or even two! In a word, in such cases the authorities essentially adopted the unjust practice of double standards.

But to return to Buondelmonte de' Buondelmonti, having accepted the imposition placed on him, he went through both the ceremony of engagement and the following phase of the contract with the girl he did not love, all the more so because he had never experienced true love, what we call 'the real thing'. Of course, the young Buondelmonte had had flirtations, and plenty of them, but the dashing knight had never known that love that sets your heart racing and keeps you awake at night and, in the end, he didn't really care that much. Perhaps these were the very thoughts passing through his mind when one morning, as he was riding through Florence on his horse, he heard someone calling him from aloft, from a window of one of the many tower-houses in the city: 'Sir! ... Messer Buondelmonte, wait please, I have something to tell you!' Buondelmonte reined in his horse and looked up to see where this woman's voice was coming from. He could not have imagined in that moment what destiny had in store for him. He saw, looking out the window, an elegantly dressed lady who was smiling at him: it was Aldrada Donati, the mother of the two beautiful girls we mentioned at the beginning of this chapter, one of whom – or perhaps both – was secretly in love with that breaker of ladies' hearts.

'Tell me, sir', continued the lady, 'what woman are you about to take to wife? I have kept this one for you!', and so say-

Fig. 19 - The church of Santo Stefano al Ponte

ing she moved aside and her place at the window was taken by one of her two gorgeous daughters, the very Beatrice who had been pining so long with love for the brave knight. It was love at first sight, head over heels. For the first time, Buondelmonte's heart gave a bound. The practised hero of so many fleeting love affairs was truly smitten by an overwhelming sentiment that he had never felt before. Nowadays all this makes us smile, because that's certainly not the way today's young people fall in love. But we have to consider that in those days, when a woman would be considered a strumpet if she dared to show even her ankle, things proceeded very differently. Often a mere glance was more eloquent than any discourse. Transfixed by this angelic vision, young Buondelmonte realised that he had finally discovered what true love was, the kind that can last a lifetime, and even beyond.

When the girl disappeared into the house and her place was taken again by her mother, the poor knight was so overcome with confusion that he was scarcely able to open his mouth to say sorrowfully. 'Madam, at this point, there's nothing else I can do ...'. The lady, however, with exquisitely feminine guile, continued insisting: 'Yes you can! Are you perhaps afraid of having to pay the penalty? I can pay that for you!' Buondelmonte was inordinately rich and definitely had no need for the mother of the girl to pay the penalty, that is the compensation, for him. Nevertheless, those words gave him the courage to put love before his sense of duty as a knight committed to another woman through a regular and official engagement. And so, he took his courage in his hands and replied: 'So be it, I love your daughter and I shall join palms with her!'

Having made this decision, Buondelmonte lost no time in putting it into action. He immediately broke off his engagement with Reparata Amidei, and very rapidly organised the wedding with the damsel who had finally succeeded in winning his heart.

On that Easter Sunday morning of the year 1216 it must indeed have been a fine sight to see the noble knight Buondelmonte making his way through the crowd, splendidly dressed in white robes and riding a snow-white palfrey, crossing the Ponte Vecchio alongside his beautiful bride to attend mass, probably in the ancient Florentine cathedral of Santa Reparata. But there was to be no happy ever after for them. On the other side of the bridge the young couple were to meet with a terrible destiny that would bring their love story to a tragic end.

In fact, a few days before, in another nearby church called Santa Maria sopra Porta – since evidently at the time churches were seen as the ideal places for hatching plots – there had been a meeting of the noble coterie of the Amidei family and its supporters, which had been offended for the second time and in an even more humiliating manner. The church on that day must have seemed like an authentic tribunal, and even the priest could hardly fail to have been in agreement with what was being planned. We can imagine with what impartiality those people, with their hearts full of rage, must have put the unwitting Buondelmonte on trial, and what punishments they were planning to inflict on him. Some suggested demanding moral reparation from him in the form of a public apology, others proposed corporal punishment in the form of flogging. However, the majority of those present felt that such punishments were far too lenient, and that he ought to be killed. It was at that very moment when the decision was made to assassinate the man who had broken his promise, that Mosca dei Lamberti, who was the most furious of all, pronounced for the first time the phrase that after more than 800 years is still so commonly used by the Florentines 'Cosa fatta, capo ha!': it was Buondelmonte's death sentence.

On Easter morning the conspirators met in the houses of the Amidei family close to the church of Santo Stefano al Ponte and, armed with weapons, awaited the arrival of Buondelmonte and his bride who on this festive occasion were sure to cross the Ponte Vecchio on their way to attend mass in the city.

And indeed, not long afterwards the young couple appeared, happy and smiling and holding hands. They moved forwards slowly, replying to the greetings of people in the crowd; after crossing the bridge they arrived at the foot of the statue of

Mars on horseback. It was at this point that Schiatta degli Uberti broke away from the crowd and struck Buondelmonte violently with a club, knocking him off his horse. Mosca dei Lamberti and Lambertuccio degli Amidei (the father of the abandoned girl) jumped on him before he had time to stand up, stabbing him repeatedly with their daggers. But the mortal blow was inflicted by the girl's uncle, the previously wounded Oddo Arrighi, and it is not unlikely that the rejected girl, possibly with inner satisfaction, witnessed the entire scene from the window of her tower-house that overlooked the site of the assault.

However, blinded by anger and the spirit of vendetta, the coterie of the Amidei had made a bad choice in the place, date, and time of the assassination. On Easter day the streets were full of people who were cheerfully making their way to the various churches to the sound of the festive bells. That large red bloodstain, in jarring contrast to the snow-white garments of the victim and the blossom of the numerous flowering trees that were in that area, could not fail to send a shudder of terrified shock through the crowds that found themselves helpless witnesses to the tragic episode and the despair of the young and now widowed bride.

Horror and malediction spread through the city like wildfire. 'They have killed Messer Buondelmonte!' was the cry that echoed through the streets, the squares, and the lanes, while from the site of the murder what ought to have been a joyful procession but was instead a dismal funeral cortege began heading towards Santa Reparata. The corpse of the young Buondelmonte was laid out on a stretcher covered with flowers, especially roses, the vermilion red of which mingled with that of the blood on the white clothes. Walking next to the stretcher, with her hair loose as a sign of grief, was the beautiful young bride supporting the head of her dead husband in a most piteous gesture. This heartrending sight moved even those citizens who had disapproved of Buondelmonte's fickle behaviour towards his first fiancée and had taken her part. Now, in the face of such atrocity and barefaced contempt for the laws of both man and God, the populace was unanimous in taking the part of the Buondelmonti, demanding that justice be done and opposing the supporters of the Amidei, the Arrighi, and all the other nobles who had shown such ferocity in planning and carrying out the cruel and bloody vendetta.

Therefore, the people applied with determination to the *podestà*, that is the governor of Florence, a certain Gherardo Rolandini from Bologna, who was in charge of the administration of justice. The instigators and perpetrators of the crime were well known to all so that no investigations were necessary. All that needed to be done was to apply the laws of the city and condemn the guilty parties without delay. This time, even if they had wanted to, the city authorities could not pretend that nothing had happened in the face of a populace that appeared to be threatening a revolt. By this time the Alberti, the Uberti, the Lamberti, the Amidei, the Fifanti, the Arrighi and their coteries realised that they had gone too far and were in grave danger. In the attempt to escape civic justice, they did something that had consequences that no one at the time could possibly have imagined, not only for the future history of Florence, but that of Italy as a whole and of Germany. It was in fact this that gave rise to the factions of the Guelphs and the Ghibellines.

What did these nobles do that was of such significance? When they realised that their lives were in danger, they decided to appeal to imperial law, which did not recognise the validity of the communal Ordinances on which the administration of justice in Florence was based, and which were drawn up and adopted without the approval of the German emperor. In a word, by failing to recognise the independence of the commune of Florence from the empire, these nobles openly joined ranks with the emperor, Frederick II, allying themselves abstractly with what would become authentic Ghibellinism. Clearly, they could not have imagined the vast political repercussions of such a gesture. All that they were concerned with at the time was to place themselves under the protection of imperial law rather than that of the commune so as to evade justice.

Prior to the assassination, the Buondelmonti had not had groups of important families or coteries to support them, to the extent that the young breaker of Florentine maidens' hearts had found himself alone in addressing vendettas. Instead, after his death everyone who was seeking justice in full respect of the civic institutions came together in his name and memory. This group then naturally found itself opposed to the nobles who in order to escape Florentine justice had sided with the Ghibelline – namely Frederick II – and ultimately had little choice but to in turn join ranks with the Guelph party, namely Otto IV who was Frederick II's enemy. This didn't mean taking the part of one emperor against another, but rather seeking in him authoritative support for the freedom of the commune of Florence to impose its own Ordinances of Justice in complete independence. The chroniclers of the time don't tell us whether or not those responsible for the tragic end to a love story that seemed to belong to the realm of fairy tale were brought to justice. Nevertheless, it seems unlikely that they would have succeeded in escaping an exemplary sentence, considering that the newborn Guelph party governed the city of Florence unchallenged for almost half a century.

To end this chapter, I should like to add a few words about Frederick II, under whose protection the assassins of Buondelmonte had placed themselves. Frederick was indeed a quite unique figure: a German emperor of Swabian blood, born to a Sicilian mother and of Oriental education and inclination. He was a Christian but was constantly surrounded and protected by a Saracen guard. He was a firm believer in astrology, and was himself an astrologer, and he surrounded himself with oriental magicians and astrologers who followed him wherever he went. It was these very astrologers who, after consulting the stars, predicted that he would die in the area of Florence. Frightened by this prediction, Frederick II always carefully avoided passing close to Florence in his continual transits between northern and southern Italy. He was convinced that if he never travelled through this area the unlucky prediction could not come true. As a result, he issued bans, orders, and decrees and promulgated laws with a view to reducing Florence to obedience, but avoided the city completely and did not even want to see its walls from a distance. Nonetheless, despite all his precautions, destiny struck and did so in exactly the way that had been predicted. However, Frederick did not die in Florence, which he never visited, but rather in an accident on 13 December 1250 in his dominions of Capitanata, to the north-west of Lucera where he and his faithful Saracens had their fortress, in a town whose name was fatal for him: Castel Fiorentino.

THE CANTO DEL DIAVOLO

The corner between Via Vecchietti and Via Strozzi in the very centre of Florence is known as the 'Canto del Diavolo' – literally 'Devil's Corner' – and this very spot is marked by a bronze copy of Giambologna's 'little devil'.

It seems that in 1245 at this very corner the Dominican friar, Pietro da Verona, was preaching to the people when the devil appeared in the form of a rearing black horse, whereupon Pietro made a sign of the cross and the devil disappeared. A similar occurrence is recorded in the background of a fresco on the facade of the beautiful little Loggia del Bigallo, on the corner between Via Calzaiuoli and Piazza San Giovanni. Once again, the episode took place during a sermon by Fra Pietro, and here too the devil appeared in the form of a rearing black horse. At the sign of the cross made by the friar, to the amazement of the crowd, the horse set off at a gallop into the air, its hoofs grazing the heads of the faithful who all loudly acclaimed the miracle, while not one was even minimally hurt.

Pietro da Verona, also known as Saint Peter Martyr, was also said to be the founder of an order known as the Compagnia Maggiore di Santa Maria, which ran a hospice for abandoned children and unwanted old people that had its premises in Via de' Calzaiuoli, not far from the loggia just mentioned. It

Fig. 20 - The 'little devil' of Giambologna

was referred to as the Bigallo after the crest showing two *galli*, or cockerels.

These were the foundations for the birth of the very old and famous Compagnia della Misericordia which still exists today in Piazza del Duomo, close to the corner with Via de' Calzaiuoli, always at the ready with its rapid ambulance service to reach any sick or wounded person in need of help.

Fig. 21 - The Loggia del Bigallo

Pietro da Verona, who was nicknamed 'Gideon's trumpet' by his contemporaries on account of his resounding sermons, was assassinated by heretical Cathari at Seveso on 6 April 1252. He was wounded in the head and, before he died, he dipped his finger in his own blood and wrote on the ground his last words 'I believe in God'. From then on, he was known in Florence as St Peter Martyr.

Fig. 22 - The loggia of the facade of Santissima Annunziata

THE SERVITES
AND SANTISSIMA ANNUNZIATA

In the year 1082 Florence suffered a long siege by the Emperor Henry IV who was encamped with his troops on an area of land known as *cafaggio* – meaning meadow – which was situated more or less on the site of what is now Piazza Santissima Annunziata. But Henry was at the head of a cobbled-together army that had nothing of the aggressive determination of the opposing Florentine forces. In addition, the muggy heat of high summer played a decisive role in draining what little drive the besiegers had left, and soon the discouraged emperor gave up the attempt and departed, abandoning many of his battle accoutrements such as tents and armour in the field.

The exultant Florentines attributed their victory to the intercession of the Madonna and built a small chapel dedicated to her on the spot where the besiegers had been. However, after a short time the people forgot about the grace received and the little chapel was left in a state of dereliction. For almost two centuries it remained neglected and forgotten, until it was almost completely overgrown by shrubs and brambles.

The Florentine army was always at war with everyone, and around the year 1230 it was besieging Siena. With the contemptuous ferocity that this army accustomed to winning habitually demonstrated towards its enemies, it took delight in

Fig. 23 - Detail of the painting by Bartolomeo, with the face of the
Madonna traditionally believed to have been painted by an angel

catapulting into the famished city chopped up pieces of donkey's carcass and similar filth. Both the pope and the emperor wanted an end to the war, but the Florentines listened to neither. Therefore, Gregory IX decided to send to Florence as a peacemaker a great preacher who was also famous as a miracle-worker, and was said to be able even to raise the dead. However, the Florentines – who when they were at war had little inclination to listen to exhortations for peace – replied sarcastically: 'For the love of God let the holy man stay where he is, in Florence he might even raise the dead and here we already have far too many of the living!'

Nevertheless, not everyone was in favour of the horror of this continual warfare and so many deaths, both because it caused suffering and famine for the poor and also because, even among the citizens that were more comfortably off, there were many people who could not put up with all this slaughter any longer. Several noble Florentines were deeply disturbed by the situation; tired of wars, slaughter and corruption, these men – who were later sanctified and called the 'seven Florentine saints' – meditated a return to prayer and to God. One day the Madonna appeared to them, dressed in black and with the appearance and attitude of Our Lady of Sorrows. After this apparition, the seven men decided to devote themselves to the service of Our Lady and created the Servants of Mary, the religious order known as the Servites, friars of the Santissima Annunziata. These seven patrician Florentines left their worldly goods, their families, and their businesses, and withdrew to a life of poverty, prayer, and penitence at the top of a mountain not far from Florence known as 'Asinario', now Monte Senario. Here they built a convent that is still there to this day, albeit much larger and altered in appearance.

It was these very friars who, descending to Florence from Monte Senario, passed along the road that is still called Via dei Servi, and saw that tiny old chapel half-hidden by the undergrowth and in a state of total dereliction. They decided to restore it and to make it their habitual stop for rest and prayer every time they entered and left the city. Later, these same friars obtained the chapel as a gift from the Bishop of Florence and founded there what was the initial nucleus of what would become over time the beautiful basilica of Santissima Annunziata.

The costs entailed in starting work on the construction of the church were sustained by the extremely wealthy brother of one of the seven founder saints, Alessandro Falconieri. Why is the basilica dedicated to Our Lady of the Annunciation and not to Our Lady of Sorrows? It seems that this change took place over time, due to the fickle character of the Florentines.

There is no doubt that, when the church was enlarged in the early fourteenth century, the place of honour on the altar at the end of the single aisle was occupied by the image of Our Lady of Sorrows. But there was another image on the rear wall, on the right before the exit from the church, that of the angel greeting Mary and announcing to her the birth of Jesus. This work was commissioned from a relatively unknown artist, a certain Bartolomeo, who nevertheless succeeded in giving his painting the most tender and mystical expression imaginable. It was one of the most beautiful images to be seen in Florence at the time, and after having said their last Hail Marys, the faithful would linger longer before this image than before that of Our Lady of Sorrows. And this devotion grew even more rapidly when the word began to go round that the face of Our Lady had not been painted by Bartolomeo but by an angel descended from heaven. Indeed, a tradition that is still very much alive among the faithful holds that the artist had already finished the work except for the face of Our Lady but, feeling himself inadequate to the task of giving an appearance to Mary, he would not dare place his brush on the place where he had to paint the face. It seemed that the work would have to be left unfinished, and the disconsolate painter fell asleep in front of his easel. Imagine his surprise when he awoke to find that the work was completed! An angel had finished the painting and the Virgin Mary finally had her face: at once sweet and grave, delicate and severe, mystically intent and gently sublime, just as we can all still see her, still in the same place inside Santissima Annunziata. Michelangelo himself, when he saw this face, was greatly struck by it and had no difficulty in accepting that it had been created through supernatural intervention.

The feast of the birth of the Virgin Mary is celebrated on 8 September, and since ancient times the cult of Our Lady has been very widespread among the Florentines, both those in the city and those living in the countryside. It was tradition that on the evening of 7 September the country farmers, accompanied by their womenfolk dressed in their finest clothes for the festivities, would come into the city, stopping on the way in Piazza Santissima Annunziata to sell the figs from their country orchards. To provide some light in the big square, they brought with them candles – protected by paper lampshades so that they would not be blown out by the wind – attached to the end of long canes. These lanterns were originally known as *fierucolone* but with the passage of time the name was transformed to *rificolone*, while the lanterns too became increasingly imaginative and colourful.

It is a very long time now since the country folk came to sell their figs in the city, but up to the end of the last century it continued to be traditional on 7 September for children accompanied by their parents to gather in the streets along the river to show off ever bigger, more original and beautiful paper lanterns, competing to show whose was the biggest and the best. But then there were also bands of little rascals armed with peashooters who tried to strike the lanterns with tiny balls of paper or putty, often succeeding in setting them alight to the obvious despair of the little lantern-holders. Now, even this tradition is disappearing and it's a real shame. Not only are the children increasingly deprived of the imaginative stimuli that are so crucial to intellectual development, but we are also progressively losing the poetry of those festivities and traditions which have always given life a special savour.

Fig. 24 - The church of Sant'Ambrogio

NAPLES HAS SAN GENNARO...
FLORENCE HAS SANT'AMBROGIO

Florence is full of miraculous images. Even in the church of Santa Trinita there is a miraculous crucifix with the head bowed. It's said that this head of Christ was originally upright, but when a great saint – St John Gualberto – decided to pardon the man who had murdered his brother, the figure on the crucifix bowed his head as a sign of approval of this gesture. So, it's not surprising that Florence also has another famous relic, although few people know about it, even among the Florentines themselves.

Let's take a look at the facts through the words of one of the most famous and trustworthy chroniclers of ancient Florence, Giovanni Villani:

In the said year of 1229, on 30 December, the feast of San Firenze, a priest from the church of Sant'Ambrogio, having said the Mass and celebrated the Sacrifice, because he was getting on in years forgot to dry the chalice properly, and it turned out that the very next day, when he took up the said chalice, he found that it contained living blood, clotted and flesh-coloured.

That elderly priest was called Uguccione and, after some uncertainty, the Benedictine nuns of Sant'Ambrogio decided to report the episode to the Bishop of Florence, Ardingo,

Fig. 25 - The tabernacle by Mino da Fiesole
inside the church of Sant'Ambrogio

who ordered the cruet in which the drops of blood had been collected to be brought to him immediately. It seemed that the bishop was concerned to sequester the relic to conceal the carelessness of the priest. However, at this point the nuns decided to apply to the Franciscan friars of Santa Croce, who had always been considered the best interpreters of the popular spirit. Indeed, news of the happening had already spread through the local district and the people were clamouring for the bishop to return the miraculous relic. The Franciscans were successful, and brought the relic back to Sant'Ambrogio in a solemn procession in which a huge crowd took part. The bishop had been greatly disturbed by the event and that night he was unable to sleep. Tossing and turning, all of a sudden he heard a voice speaking to him emphatically and saying 'Naked you received me and naked you returned me.' At this point he realised that the voice of God was alluding to the absence of a reliquary to more fittingly hold the blood produced in what everyone now openly proclaimed to be a 'miracle'.

The reliquary was duly made, and became ever more beautiful as a result of the continual embellishments made to it, especially after the Signoria of Florence entrusted the church of Sant'Ambrogio – which by then was known as the 'church of the miracle' – to the noble Guild of Judges and Notaries. Later the nuns of Sant'Ambrogio commissioned from one of the greatest sculptors of the time, Mino da Fiesole, the magnificent tabernacle that can still be admired today in the Chapel of the Miracle.

In the same chapel is a large fresco of the procession of the miracle painted shortly afterwards by Cosimo Rosselli. Here, to make the point that belief in the miracle was not restricted to the people but also extended to influential figures and leading intellectuals, he included amidst the astonished and enraptured crowd the portraits of several of his contemporaries, the great humanists Pico della Mirandola, Marsilio Ficino and Agnolo Poliziano. Obviously, this was a case of artistic licence on the part of the painter, since the miracle had taken place over two centuries before his time.

Fig. 26 - Miniature showing the interior
of a fourteenth-century Florentine hospital, with the patients
in their beds, the doctors, and the nurses

FLORENCE: TOP IN THE RANKING FOR HOSPITALS TOO

In the Middle Ages there was no city that did not have problems of hygiene. We have to bear in mind that, while today our houses are all equipped with waste pipes running into drainage channels, sewers, or septic tanks, in those days all the waste ended up running down open sewers in the street. Household waste too was not transported to special dumps, but piled up in the street where it was picked over by rats, dogs, and other animals. During the winter, ice and rain made the situation slightly more tolerable, but in the summer ... You can probably imagine the terrible stench of rotting organic matter and excrement which, apart from being extremely unpleasant was also the source of drastic problems of health and hygiene. This is another reason why plagues were so frequent in the Middle Ages, to the point of even decimating the population. And even when there were no plagues, the people were afflicted by numerous diseases of different kinds caused by the lack of cleanliness. Before the time of public hospitals, health care was provided by the convents and monasteries, although obviously they were only able to assist a limited number of people. As a result, when the population of a settlement grew to the size of a city, the need to provide appropriate healthcare facilities became pressing. This happened in Florence in the fourteenth century, when the huge growth of the population made the question of an appropriate hospital structure extremely urgent.

Several hospitals were built in Florence at this time, but the most striking example is that of the hospital of Santa Maria founded by Folco Portinari, father of the famous Beatrice who was beloved by the great poet Dante. This is the oldest hospital in Florence, and one of the oldest in Europe. It was not located exactly where the present hospital of Santa Maria Nuova now stands in the square of the same name. The old hospital was on the opposite side of the square, between Via Sant' Egidio and Via Folco Portinari, where the old church of Santa Maria still exists together with the convent of the Oblates, now housing the city library on several floors. The appellative 'Nuova' was added to 'Santa Maria when the hospital was transferred from its original premises to where it is now. But, as we said, this was not by any means the only hospital in Florence: the statistics provided by the historic chronicler Villani record that in 1340 Florence already had no less than thirty hospitals serving a population of 90,000, with a total of over 1,000 beds available. So, there was a hospital bed available for every 90 inhabitants; this was a social achievement that not only placed Florence in the vanguard for hospital care at the time, but also a ratio that it is no exaggeration to claim that very few cities – perhaps none at all – can boast even today.

And that's not all. The Florentine hospitals had facilities that no other city in the world possessed. At that time, sick people were stretched out on long wooden pallets, dozens of them on the same one. In Florence, on the contrary, each patient had their own bed, complete with pillow, with a pillow case that could be changed, as well as their own fork and beaker. Such a 'luxury' was genuinely unheard-of, and could very well be seen as a feather in the cap of the city's healthcare, especially when combined with another marvel that was the pride and joy of these hospitals: each patient had their own chamber pot!

The staff in charge of the treatment of the sick were also the best that the medical science of the time could supply: the most diligent of doctors would examine their patients on a daily basis, with the assistance of qualified nursing staff. There were also other assistants who were in charge of changing the bed linen, making the beds, and sweeping out the wards.

And so, ought we to be envious of how hospital care functioned in those far-off times? Well, yes and no, considering that for diseases of the liver the most advanced medical 'science' of the time prescribed quartering a live dog and applying it, still warm, to the area of pain ...

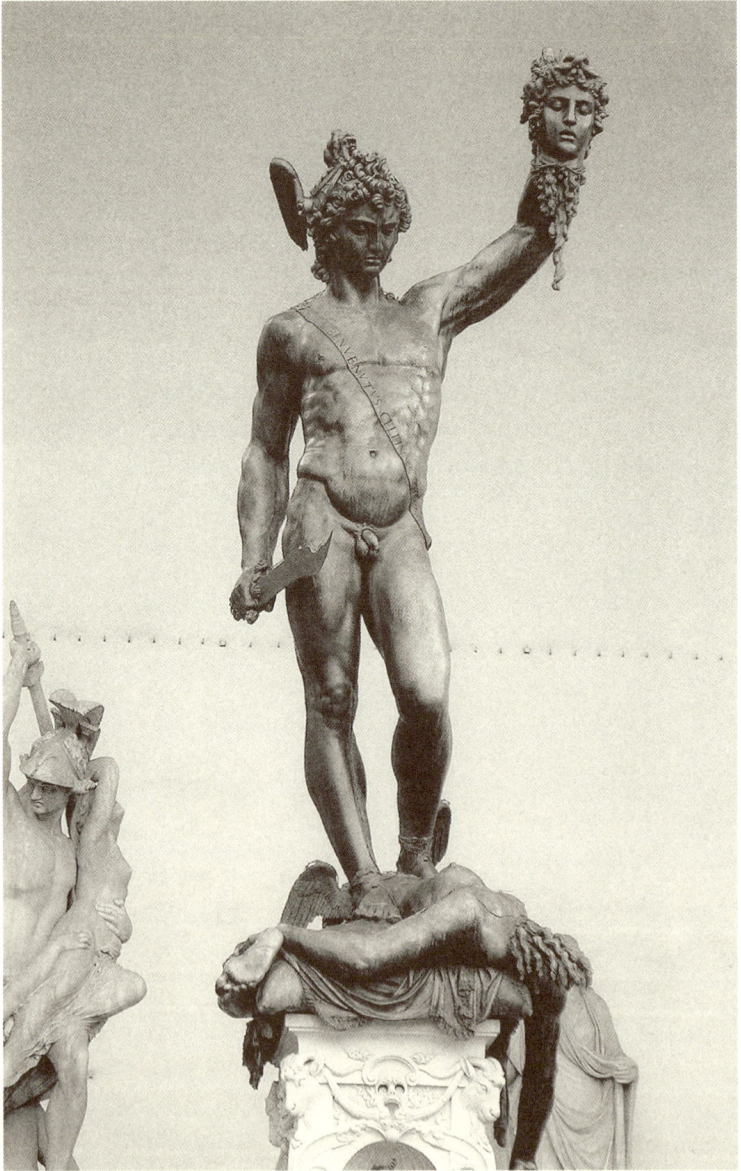

Fig. 27 - The *Perseus* of Benvenuto Cellini

OUTLANDISH, A MONEYLENDER AND A TRICKSTER, BUT ALSO... A SUBLIME ARTIST!

In a house at no. 29 Via della Pergola (which used to be called Via del Canto al Rosaio) was the house and workshop of the great Benvenuto Cellini, the goldsmith and sculptor who, among other works, created the *Perseus* that can be admired in Piazza della Signoria.

Cellini was indeed a strange character. No one who stops to look at the bronze bust of him set up at the midpoint of the Ponte Vecchio would ever imagine what kind of man – as well as artist – he actually was. He lent money at interest, although it has to be said that this appears to have fairly common among great artists, and it is said that even Giotto spent more time collecting interest on the florins he loaned than working on his paintings!

If he was not paid punctually, Benvenuto Cellini was more than capable of brandishing his arquebus and demanding payment under threat. It's also said that he ran a bookie shop, taking bets on the gender of babies that were due to be born. There were also spiteful tongues that accused him of cheating, and it appears that he exploited a personal and highly efficient channel of information about births that, unbeknownst to the betters, had already taken place. Apropos this, a very serious charge was brought against him by no less than the Grand

Duchess Eleonora of Toledo, who had made one such wager with him. However, before placing all the blame on Cellini we have to ask ourselves whether it may not have been the grand duchess herself to launch this calumny against him in the wake of the popular outcry accusing him of cheating. The fact is that there was a precedent which could have induced the wife of the lord of Florence, Cosimo, to take revenge on Cellini. Shortly before, while visiting the artist's workshop, Eleonora had seen four statuettes that were to have been part of the pedestal for the statue of *Perseus* that he was working on. The grand duchess was so entranced by these statuettes of Jupiter, Minerva, Mercury, and Danaë, that she wanted to have them at all costs. But Benvenuto refused to sell them to her. We can imagine how furious this great lady must have been with the artist, and this could even suggest a wily feminine vendetta on her part when, after having wagered with Cellini on the gender of a new baby, she accused him of having cheated by replacing the boy in the cradle with a girl just so that he would win the bet.

The four statuettes that the Grand Duchess Eleonora had set her heart on are the very same that Cellini then set into the pedestal of his *Perseus*, where we can all still admire them. As regards this magnificent and famous statue, which represents Perseus just after he has cut off the head of the Medusa as a symbol of justice, it is interesting to relate the vicissitudes that the artist lived through in the course of its casting, which was carried out personally by the great artist with just a few assistants. He narrowly escaped both his house and his workshop being destroyed by fire following an accident which, as usual, they tried to blame on Benvenuto himself. The usual malignant rumours began to circulate that there was a risk that the casting of the *Perseus* would fail because the artist had tried to skimp on the bronze alloy, using too little tin in proportion to the copper, which cost much less. The malicious gossips promptly relayed this accusation to the Grand Duke Cosimo I de' Medici, who had commissioned the statue from Cellini the year before (this was 1545). In effect, the grand duke failed to show any great trust in the artist, since he immediately ordered the *bargello* (police chief) to send a squad of policemen round to Cellini's house, with the order to arrest him if anything went wrong with the casting.

We can easily imagine Cellini's state of mind when, with the police waiting on the threshold, he realised that the casting of the *Perseus* was indeed at risk of not succeeding.

This is how things went, according to Cellini's own account in his *Autobiography*:

> *The logs of pine were heaped in, and, what with the unctuous resin of the wood and the good draught I had given, my furnace worked so well that I was obliged to rush from side to side to keep it going. The labour was more than I could stand; yet I forced myself to strain every nerve and muscle. To increase my anxieties, the workshop took fire, and we were afraid lest the roof should fall upon our heads; while, from the garden, such a storm of wind and rain kept blowing in, that it perceptibly cooled the furnace. Battling thus with all these untoward circumstances for several hours, and exerting myself beyond even the measure of my powerful constitution, I could at last bear up no longer, and a sudden fever, of the utmost possible intensity, attacked me. I felt absolutely obliged to go and fling myself upon my bed.*

And so, as a result of his utter exhaustion, Benvenuto, really did risk seeing his statue lost. The raging fever that kept him confined to his bed was apparently caused simply by this effort, in addition to the stress of an extraordinary nervous tension. This theory is borne out by the words uttered by the artist himself in the presence of his housekeeper: the good *mona* Fiore di Castel del Rio who, on hearing her master cry 'I shall not be alive tomorrow' broke down in tears. To make things worse, one of Benvenuto's assistants then came into the room to give him the worst of news: 'O Benvenuto! your statue is spoiled, and there is no hope whatever of saving it.' These words struck Cellini like a whiplash, like the strongest of medicines. Just a few seconds before he had appeared to be at death's door and now, after letting out a loud cry, he starting dressing himself as fast as he could, punching and kicking any of the lads or maidservants who tried to help him, crying out like one possessed 'Ah! traitors! enviers! This is an act of treason, done by intentional malice!'

And so Benvenuto rushed back to his workshop and found that the metal was all caked, and so he sent his assistants to take a pile of oak wood, which was better than any other type of wood to make the fire burn hot. Whereupon Cellini's own description continues, 'oh, how the cake began to stir beneath that awful heat, to glow and sparkle in a blaze!' And so the metal began to run, but not as rapidly as was required. More tin had to be added to the alloy, but there was none in the workshop. Cellini did not give up. He had his assistants bring to the workshop the dishes, bowls and all the other objects made of tin that there were in the house, in all around two hundred items. And now we let Benvenuto Cellini recount the conclusion in his own words:

This expedient succeeded, and every one could now perceive that my bronze was in most perfect liquefaction, and my mould was filling; whereupon they all with heartiness and happy cheer assisted and obeyed my bidding, while I, now here, now there, gave orders, helped with my own hands, and cried aloud: 'O God! Thou that by Thy immeasurable power didst rise from the dead, and in Thy glory didst ascend to heaven!'; even thus in a moment my mould was filled; and seeing my work finished, I fell upon my knees, and with all my heart gave thanks to God. After all was over, I turned to a plate of salad on a bench there, and ate with hearty appetite, and drank together with the whole crew. Afterwards I retired to bed, healthy and happy, and slept as sweetly as though I had never had an illness in the world.

Fig. 28 - The Guelph and Ghibelline merlons of Palazzo Vecchio

The Only 'Eagle' That Was Not Devoured by the Florentine Lions

We've already talked about the Florentine symbols of the eagle and the lion: the eagle represented imperial power, that is the oppressor supported by the Ghibellines, while the lion was for Florence the symbol of the city's freedom from the yoke of the empire.

However, when in 1470 the Ghibellines were definitively driven out of Florence and Guelph power was established unchallenged, all the Ghibelline symbols of imperial power were removed forever from the city. So, why is there still a solitary eagle bearing a green dragon between its talons clearly visible among the coats of arms of the Guelph republic running along beneath the battlements of Palazzo Vecchio? Why has that single, solitary eagle survived among the numerous lions of the old Florentine Republic? There really are a great many lions that could have devoured it, right there in their den in Piazza della Signoria, where there are lions everywhere! As well as the famous lion known as the *Marzocco* by the great Donatello, there are another two lions that appear to be keeping guard on the steps of the Loggia dell'Orcagna, also known as the Loggia dei Lanzi, where there is another lavish lion decoration with no less than three lions for each of the columns. Another two lions flank the frieze with the monogram of Cristo Re above the main entrance to the Palazzo della Signoria, along with a veritable pride of lions, whole or heads only, that we can admire prowling around the vast chambers inside the palace. Practically wherever you turn your gaze while standing in Piazza della Signoria you have the sensation of being in the middle of a menagerie, and there are more lions adorning the inner cornice of the loggia, where in the olden days coloured flags were hung during the public ceremonies.

In such a patently Guelph Florence, it is really hard to understand at first glance why that eagle – generally a symbol of the detested imperial enemy – was not eliminated. It seems almost incredible, but the truth is that this red eagle with the green dragon between its talons is actually a coat of arms of the 'lions' faction, namely the Guelphs!

To explain this little mystery better to the visitor, we have to take another leap backwards in time to the year 1260 when, after the battle of Montaperti, it was the Guelphs who were driven out of Florence by the Ghibelline victors. The exiled Guelphs sought refuge and protection first with Pope Urban IV and then with Pope Clement IV, who were both French and anti-imperial. The popes gave them money and many other benefits, and when these political refugees asked how they could display their gratitude, Clement replied that the only thing he wanted as recompense was that they should always remain faithful to him. The pope went on to add that, as a symbol of such loyalty, he would be greatly pleased if the Guelph party would adopt the coat of arms of his family: a red eagle on a white field holding a green dragon between its claws. Just a few years later, the Florentine political situation completely reversed the fate of the two factions: the Guelphs returned definitively to power, while the Ghibellines were banished. At this point the Guelph party remembered their promise to the pope and included his arms among the other Guelph escutcheons.

102

However, when all these things happened, the beautiful town hall of Florence, Palazzo della Signoria (which was only later called Palazzo Vecchio) did not yet exist. Construction did not begin until thirty years later, in 1301. Dante Alighieri, who was thirty-six at the time, was able to see only the beginning of the work since a year later he was banished from the city and condemned to permanent exile, accused of corruption and embezzlement, and of hostility towards both Pope Boniface VII and the brother of the King of France, and paladin of the Guelphs, Charles of Valois. In truth, Dante's only fault was his strenuous defence of the interests of the Florentine Republic when, while holding office as prior, he consistently opposed the absurd and insistent demands for soldiers and gold florins for their wars made on Florence by both the pope and Charles of Valois. It was a series of *Nihil fiat* refusals that cost Dante the exile that led to his dying far from his beloved homeland – in 1321 in Ravenna – without ever seeing Florence again. Apropos Palazzo Vecchio, it is said that while in exile, every time that Dante met someone from Florence he would enquire 'Is the Palazzo of the priors coming along nicely?'

The very first name of Palazzo Vecchio was indeed Palazzo dei Priori, since it was built specifically to accommodate the council of the priors, and only later became the Palazzo della Signoria. Florence had never before had an appropriate premises where the priors, who were elected by the people to govern the city, could meet to discuss the application of the laws. Previously the priors would meet in different places, wherever they had sufficient space at disposal. Then, as it was in Dante's time, they had settled in the Torre della Castagna, which still exists not far from Piazza della Signoria, on the corner between Via de' Magazzini and Via Dante Alighieri. However, as time passed, even these premises no longer seemed appropriate to the grandeur of Florence, and so it was decided to build the large and beautiful palace to a design by Arnolfo di Cambio. But this was no simple matter, because two major problems immediately emerged and it was many years before these could be solved and the first stone laid. The first problem was this, what was the point in building a beautiful palazzo if no one would be able to admire it? Today's tourists who are able to appreciate the huge expanse of Piazza della Signoria cannot even imagine how much it cost the old Florentine Republic to carve out that vast square. To get an idea, we have to consider that in the fourteenth century the area now occupied by the square and by Palazzo Vecchio itself was a maze of narrow alleys bristling with tower-houses. Even if all the houses in the area necessary to build the palazzo were bought up and razed to the ground, who would have been able to admire it from the narrow alleyways all around that occupied the rest of what is now the square? And so it became necessary – at a financial outlay we can easily imagine – to expropriate a vast area of the city, comprising all the houses that then had to be demolished. Only then could this fine palazzo be built that would be truly worthy of the city of Florence.

However, as we said, there was also a second problem: the place chosen for the construction of the 'Palagio dei Priori per lo Comune et popolo di Firenze' was the very area in which the houses of the Uberti family were located. Since the Uberti were 'rebels against Florence and Ghibellines to boot' the palazzo could not be built on that accursed spot. To literally 'get round' this problem, other neighbouring houses belonging to the Foraboschi family had to be bought up, including a tower known as the 'Vacca' which was more than 29 metres high. This tower still exists, incorporated into the tower of Palazzo Vecchio, and it also gave its name to the street in front, which is still called Via Vacchereccia. The architect Arnolfo di Cambio used the solid shaft of this tower as the buttress for the facade and the substructure of the present tower, which for this reason was not built on top of the palazzo but, resting on such a solid base, was able to soar daringly high above the gallery supported on brackets. No one had ever before seen a tower with a projecting balcony like that of Arnolfo, who sadly died before he was able to see it finished.

The concealed presence of the Vacca tower within the palace also provides the answer to the question that many tourists ask as to why the windows of the palace on the side of the tower are blind. This is no longer a mystery. To avoid the detestable site of the erstwhile Uberti houses, the entire palazzo was asymmetrical. Only the genius of the architect and sculptor from Colle Val d'Elsa – who from then on decided to call himself 'Maestro Arnolfo di Fiorenza' – succeeded in resolving even this 'political' problem in the best possible way by resorting to the harmony of the golden proportion, an architectural rule that was conceived in ancient Greece. The golden proportion, often referred to as the 'golden ratio' was widely used in the past after its rediscovery by Arnolfo. It is based on a simple formula: given a measurement corresponding to 10, this should be divided into two segments with respective measurements of 6.18 and 3.82. And, lo and behold, these are exactly the proportions into which the tower of Palazzo Vecchio divides the rest of the facade!

The building of the palazzo continued, with successive additions, up to the year 1340. It is a typical mediaeval construction in rusticated ashlar, almost a fortress, and is one of the finest examples of the style that later acquired the disparaging label of 'Gothic'. The tower was finished in 1310 and was equipped with an enormous bell, so heavy that to ring it called for the joint efforts of no less than twelve men! However, this bell was then replaced with another cast in 1322 by the Sienese master Pietro di Lando, who installed it in the tower with 'such fine and subtle artifice' that it could be set in motion by just two people and then required only one to ring it at full peal, while the sound could be heard throughout the city and at a radius of 13 miles in the hinterland. This is the very bell that we can still see at the top of this truly strange and very special tower.

The visitor admiring Palazzo Vecchio often fails to note a detail that is a true mystery: the merlons of the battlements at the level of the gallery are Guelph – which is logical considering that Florence was Guelph at the time, and the Ghibellines had been definitively beaten and driven out. So, how can we explain the presence of typically Ghibelline merlons at the top of the tower? There are no historic documents that provide an explanation of this enigma, which seems destined to remain such. It has even been suggested that the contemporary presence of Guelph and Ghibelline merlons was to symbolically represent the desired pacification between the two factions. But this explanation doesn't stand up. It would have been extremely out of character for the pugnacious Guelphs to make such a conciliatory gesture towards the detested Ghibellines, whom they defined as 'unworthy to be called citizens, or Christians, or neighbours' and hence considered devoid of all dignity and rights and deserving to be ruthlessly suppressed! Perhaps this fierce hatred was further exacerbated by the searing memory of the ignominious episode that had taken place half a century earlier when, during the historic Battle of Montaperti, the Ghibellines committed the most odious betrayal that could be imagined against the Guelphs, resulting in a fratricidal massacre. Given all this, a gesture of political conciliation is unthinkable, while on the other hand no one has ever succeeded in finding a plausible or even simply feasible justification for the mystery of these merlons.

When the Florentine Republic came to an end, in the time of Cosimo I the palace known as Palazzo della Signoria

106

was used as the seat of Medici government, and it was therefore in the Renaissance that the interior rooms were radically transformed to become the impressive salons that we can see now, including the magnificent Salone dei Cinquecento which hosted the seat of the Italian government in the nineteenth century when Florence became capital of Italy.

Fig. 29 – The panel that Giotto sculpted for his belltower,
showing a shepherd with his sheep and the famous
dog that was Giotto's childhood friend

GIOTTO'S PUPPY

Between 1283 and 1330, that is in the space of just 47 years, Florence went through a period of unbelievable growth. In 1283 the city had 45,000 inhabitants, but by 1330 it had no less than 100,000 inside the city walls and another 80,000 in the hinterland.

This was a veritable golden age for Florence. Historic documents demonstrate that the money entering the municipal coffers at the time amounted to no less than 400,000 florins a year, while normal annual expenses were no more than 40,000 florins. This explains why Florence was so rich that it could sustain financial costs that could not be rivalled by any other city. Indeed, for the commune of Florence expense was no object, especially when it came to making the city more beautiful and impressive in the eyes of the world. It must also have been very noisy in Florence at that time, since substantially the city must have been one huge building site. Suffice it to think that in the short span of 24 years between 1278 and 1301, worksites were opened for the following constructions: Santa Maria Novella; the enlargement of Santa Croce; the enlargement of the grain market of Orsanmichele with the building of warehouses; the decoration of the Baptistery of San Giovanni with beautiful white marble from Luni and green from Prato; the start of construction of Santa Maria del Fiore, the new cathedral to replace the ancient Santa Reparata; and Palazzo della Signoria, in addition to numerous hospitals and the enlargement of those already in existence, including that of Santa Maria founded by Folco Portinari, which we mentioned in another chapter.

So, the building operations set in motion by the city authorities and the guilds in this period were numerous and important. Even after the apocalyptic flood of 1333, the Florentines did not lose heart. They waited until the waters had withdrawn and then, like an army of willing ants, set about repairing what had been damaged and then turned to important new works. For instance, it was in the very aftermath of this tragic flood that work was begun on the famous belltower, the pride and joy of Florence, conceived to complete the magnificent complex of the cathedral of Santa Maria del Fiore.

Giotto was already getting on in years when he was called upon to design and build what perhaps continues to be the most famous of his works, even though it was finished by other artists after his death. Despite being no longer young, Giotto threw himself into the construction of the belltower with a truly youthful energy and the greatest enthusiasm. He even abandoned his habitual paintbrush to take up hammer and chisel, and actually carved some of the lowest row of bas-reliefs, copies of which still adorn the belltower below the first cornice, while the originals can be admired in the Museo del Duomo. Giotto worked on the tower up to his death in 1337, when the building had reached the level of the first storey. The works were then continued by Andrea Pisano, who completed the second storey, whereas the last three storeys were completed by Francesco Talenti. Following his own inspired personal interpretation of Giotto's design, Talenti altered the belltower by adding the windows that were not in Giotto's project: two double-arched windows on each side on the third and fourth storeys and a single triple-arched window on the fifth storey. This modification was made to progressively lighten the weight due to the great height (nearly 85 metres). Few people know about another important change made to the original design by Talenti. Giotto had planned to complete his tower with the typical spire of Gothic belltowers, but Talenti decided to replace it with the very fine cornice that we can all admire and that conceals from sight the low roof of the tower, with a slope just sufficient to allow for the necessary runoff of rainwater.

The belltower is square in shape, with the sides measuring around 15 metres, and reaches a total height of 84.7 metres. The walls are 3.6 metres thick at the base and 3.1 on the upper levels, which are reached by a characteristic helical staircase. Looking at the lower section of the belltower, beneath the first cornice, one can see a series of hexagonal marble bas-reliefs, some of which were sculpted by Giotto himself, as already mentioned. These include a panel showing a shepherd with his flock and, also clearly visible, his dog. Evidently, although he was in his sixties and famous, he had never forgotten that little dog who had filled his childhood years as a shepherd boy with so much love and joy. So, when he had the chance to create the bas-reliefs for his belltower, he grasped this as the perfect opportunity to honour the memory of his four-legged friend, whose image would thus live on in stone down the centuries to be admired by everyone who passed by.

With a flight of fancy, we can attempt to go back in time by around seven centuries, and find ourselves in the Florentine countryside of Vicchio in Mugello around the year 1275. In a grassy clearing bordering one of the dense forests of tall pines that – unlike now – cloaked this part of Tuscany at the time, a young shepherd boy is taking his flock to pasture. It's hot and the lad sits down on a stone to rest, while his lively dog runs

111

hither and thither shepherding the flock. The shepherd boy, a lad of about eight or nine, finds on the ground the remains of a fire that has gone out and instinctively picks up a piece of charcoal and, to pass the time, begins drawing on the stone the head of one of his sheep that is grazing nearby. Just then a man on horseback passes by and, perhaps curious to see what the boy is drawing, comes closer to take a look. When he sees the sketch on the stone he is very impressed, and gets off his horse to make a better appraisal of the artistic energy and the sureness of the hand. The man realises that the lad has a great artistic talent and immediately goes to speak about it to his father. This man was the famous Florentine painter Cimabue, while the shepherd boy was none other than Giotto, who was born in precisely this same area, in Vespignano.

Cimabue took Giotto under his wing and brought him to Florence where he became his best pupil. It was in Cimabue's workshop that Giotto learnt the rudiments of painting and art, and developed an extraordinary artistic talent. But what happened to the little dog who looked after the sheep? That dog was Giotto's best friend and he did not want to be separated from him, and so the dog came to Florence with his young master and he too began to frequent the famous workshop of Cimabue. As we know, the Florentines have always had a caustic wit, and the story goes that in this case too they lived up to their reputation. It seems that the rumour began to circulate in the city that the great Cimabue had a new pupil in his workshop, and that this pupil was . . . a dog!

As we have seen, Giotto was a great architect as well as a sculptor and, first and foremost, a sublime painter. Unfortunately, he did not leave as many traces in Florence as he did in other Italian cities. In addition to the famous *Ognissanti Madonna*, a tempera on panel conserved in the Uffizi, Giotto also executed a cycle of frescoes illustrating the life of

112

St Francis in Santa Croce, although unfortunately these were ruined by a series of irresponsible alterations and restorations carried out in the eighteenth century. The people who carried out these disastrous alterations probably didn't realise that the frescoes were by Giotto, since they chose to sacrifice the pictorial cycle to Baroque 'embellishments, which also involved the insertion of several large funerary monuments in the masonry of the nave. To do this they had to open great breaches in the frescoed walls, and the stonecarvers and builders caused irreparable damage. Giotto's paintings shattered beneath the relentless blows of hammers and chisels, falling to the ground in a cloud of dust and flaked plaster. The little that remained was covered by a layer of plaster and painted over. Fortunately, a recent restoration operation, carried out with due respect for the art, discovered the frescoes underneath the paintwork and a painstaking cleaning operation brought back to light the few areas that had escaped destruction: these consist of sections of background and parts of figures, so that the visitor to Santa Croce has to employ a good deal of imagination to try to reconstruct the lost beauty of the original composition.

We can certainly say that Giotto was unlucky with frescoes, and we with him since we have been deprived of many of his masterpieces. There is in fact another fresco cycle by this great artist that was ruined by disastrous restorations, but we will look into this in a later chapter dealing with the Palazzo del Bargello.

It's said, albeit without any supporting historic documentation, that Giotto also won a competition announced by Pope Boniface VIII for certain paintings in the Vatican, simply by tracing on parchment with a brush dipped in red ink a circle so perfect that it seemed drawn with a compass. This story has come down to us as the famous episode of Giotto's 'O'. The only fact supporting this anecdote is that Giotto was commissioned by Boniface VIII to execute the *Navicella*, or Boat, of the Church, and on the same occasion also painted a picture showing the pope announcing the 'great pardon', namely the Jubilee of 1300!

Another anecdote relates that a prince once asked Giotto to fresco his palace. It was a very hot summer and the prince who saw the artist working, covered in sweat and standing on scaffolding, said to him 'If I were you, I wouldn't work on this scaffolding in this terrible heat!' To which Giotto swiftly replied, 'And if I were you, I wouldn't either!'

A FASCINATING GLIMPSE INTO THE PAST

What follows is a list of contents of the meals to be consumed during Holy Week, leading up to Easter, taken from the 'household book' of a Florentine family at the time of Giotto and Dante.

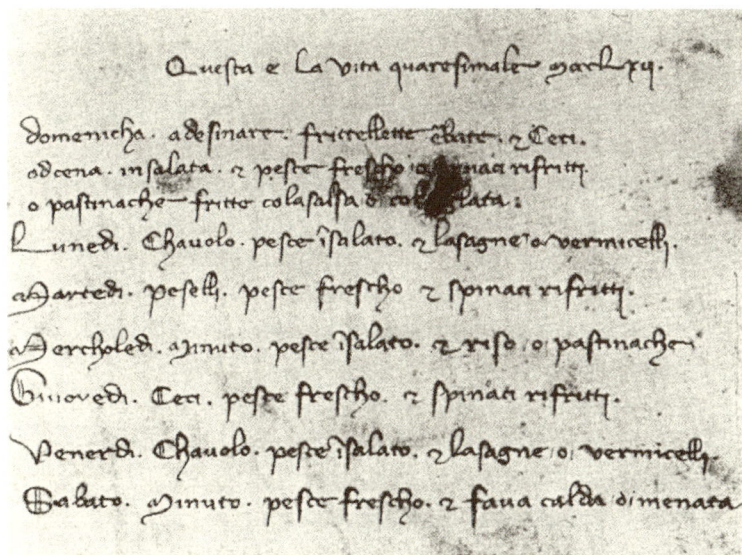

Fig. 30 - List of contents of the meals to be consumed during Holy Week, taken from the 'household book' of a fourteenth-century Florentine family

Here is the list as it was written, where xxxxx indicates words that are illegible or untranslatable into modern Italian:

Questa è la vita quaresimale xxxxx

Domenica a desinare frittellette, xxxxx, ceci.
A cena insalata, pesce frescho o spinaci rifritti o pastinache* fritto con la salsa o col xxxxx
Lunedi. Chavolo.** Pesce salato. Lasagne o vermicelli.
Martedi. peselli, pesce frescho, spinaci rifritti.
Mercoledi. Minuto pesce salato. Riso o pastinache.
Giovedi. Ceci, pesce frescho, spinaci rifritti.
Venerdi. Chavolo. Pesce salato. Lasagne o vermicelli.
Sabato. Minuto pesce frescho, fava calda dimenata.

This is Lenten fare xxxxx

Sunday at lunch small fritters, xxxxx, chick peas.

Dinner: salad, fresh fish, refried spinach [already fried and reheated] or fried parsnips with sauce or with xxxxx

Tuesday: cabbage, salted fish. Lasagna-type pasta or spaghetti.

Tuesday: peas, fresh fish, refried spinach.

Wednesday: small salted fish [such as anchovies]. Rice or parsnips.

Thursday: chick peas, fresh fish, refried spinach.

Friday: cabbage, salted fish. Lasagna-type pasta or spaghetti.

Saturday: small fresh fish [fish for frying], hot broad bean puree.

116

* *Pastinache*: it is not absolutely certain what foodstuff this refers to, but it was definitely something suitable for frying. It seems very likely that it was the vegetable now known as *pastinaca* (parsnip) which belongs to the *Umbelliferae* family. It has a long, fleshy, cream-coloured taproot (like a carrot) and is still widely used in cookery. In many parts of Italy, the term *pastinaca* and variants of the same is actually used in dialect to refer to the carrot. It seems much less likely that it referred to the fish similar to the ray also called *pastinaca*, but very rarely used as food.

** *Chavolo* (cabbage): in the ancient Tuscan vernacular, and in Florence in particular, possibly also on account of echoes of the Etruscan language, words such as *cavolo* were pronounced with a soft, aspirated 'c': substantially *cavolo* was pronounced *havolo*. To ensure that the word was pronounced correctly, the old Tuscans began to add a 'h' to the spelling: *chavolo*. The same happened with the word for fresh, *fresco*, which was written *frescho*.

CURIOUS FACTS

It is also curious to note that, at this time – between the thirteenth and fourteenth centuries – at meals it was the custom to eat first what for us would be a second course, whereas our modern first course (soup, pasta, or rice) was served as a second.

Fig. 31 - Historic football players in a typical scene from the game

TO BE STRUCK ON THE HEAD
BY TWO HAMMERS
FOR ALL ETERNITY

The Basilica of Santa Croce in the namesake square in Florence would not appear to the eyes of visitors in all its magnificence had it not been for a Franciscan friar who contended at length with his fellow friars so that the little convent in which they lived, and the small adjacent church, might be given an appearance more fitting for the 'house of God'.

The friar's name was Giovenale degli Ughi and he belonged to a noble Florentine family. However, he did not live to see his dream come true, since he died before the first stone of the splendid expansion project was laid. To make up for it, he does now rest in one of the sepulchres of the glorious temple he had so yearned for. But . . . does he really rest in peace? Given the architectural result he achieved, one would certainly hope so. Instead, according to his fellow friars he ought to be in hell, serving a terrible, eternal sentence.

So what is this about? To understand we have to be aware that there was great rivalry in those times between the erudite Dominican friars of Santa Maria Novella – who had considerable revenues at their disposal to continually enlarge and embellish their church and convent – and the poor Franciscan friars of Santa Croce who – on the example of St Francis of Assisi – had never aspired to do anything that would not be in perfect harmony with the dictates of poverty and humility of their strict Rule. So, unlike the Dominicans, the Franciscans continued to live in their primitive little convent, using the small church for the celebration of mass and the other religious functions. However, they preferred to deliver their sermons in the huge paved square in front of the church, addressing the people in the open air following the example of St Francis.

But brother Giovenale degli Ughi didn't see it that way, and in 1285 he forcefully proposed the enlargement of the church to his fellow friars, arguing that while it was true that to obey the Rule one had to be poor, it did not follow that God too should be poor, in such a miserable 'house' that was absolutely unworthy of him. As can be imagined, a lengthy and heated dispute broke out between a group of Giovenale's fellow friars who did not agree with his reasoning, and another group that was in favour. In the end the group supporting brother Giovenale prevailed, and the design for the appropriate enlargement of the church-convent complex was duly entrusted to Arnolfo di Cambio. Arnolfo began work in May 1295, but brother Giovenale had died in the meantime. The night after his death, one of the friars belonging to the group that had opposed him saw him in a dream in which he was being condemned to the cruellest punishment for having deviated from the dictates of the Franciscan Rule: poor Giovenale was being struck on the head by two heavy hammers, and would continue to suffer this punishment for all eternity. And, just by coincidence, the hammers were of exactly the same type as those used by the stonebreakers who were just starting work on the new church.

We should also clarify that the facade of Santa Croce, like that of the cathedral, is not the original but a nineteenth-century addition in neo-Gothic style, and the same is true of the belltower. The interior of the basilica was still the original one when Giotto painted his frescoes, but was then altered in 1560 by Georgio Vasari, who undoubtedly respected the paintings that were damaged only in the later remodelling operations of the eighteenth century.

Many illustrious and famous people are buried in Santa Croce, including the great Michelangelo Buonarroti. In the first cloister adjacent to the church is the beautiful chapel of the Pazzi family, built in 1430 by Filippo Brunelleschi.

CURIOUS FACTS

Towards the middle of the fourteenth century the city was divided into four 'quarters' – three to the north of the Arno and one to the south – to replace the previous division into *sestieri*, or sixths. This unwittingly also laid the foundations for the famous Florentine historic football, which is still played today in Piazza Santa Croce, saving exceptional suspensions, on the feast of St John the Baptist, the patron saint of Florence. A small tournament is played between the teams from Santa Maria Novella, San Giovanni, Santa Croce and Santo Spirito, with preliminary matches on the two Sundays preceding and the final game on 24 June, feast of St John.

Fig. 32 - The old Loggia del Grano, now the church of Orsanmichele

HISTORICAL TITBITS

THE BUTCHERS OF THE BARGELLO

Close to Piazza della Signoria, in Via dei Calzaiuoli, stands the beautiful church of Orsanmichele. Before this building was transformed into a church, it was used as a granary to store the stocks of wheat that the commune distributed to the people in times of famine. As was only to be expected when the people were starving, this distribution did not take place in a calm and organised manner, and brawls and fights were frequent. The city authorities were always afraid that such riots might light the fuse of a revolt against the institutions, a fear that was very real at the time. For this reason, the distribution of the wheat always took place under the surveillance of the Capitano del Popolo and his henchmen. Also stationed on the site on such occasions were a couple of butchers equipped with hatchets and chopping-blocks, always at the ready, on orders from the Capitano del Popolo, to chop off the hand or foot of anyone found guilty of disturbance or of inciting the crowd against the city government.

THE LOGGIA DEL PORCELLINO

Between Via Por Santa Maria and Via Porta Rossa stands the Loggia del Cinghiale, named after the fountain located

Fig. 33 - The wild boar by Pietro Tacca, known as the 'Porcellino'

there featuring the statue of a wild boar in bronze by the sculptor Pietro Tacca. However, from the very beginning the Florentines have referred to this loggia, incorrectly, as that of the 'Porcellino', or piglet, and even now continue to insist on doing so. The loggia now hosts a market selling articles made of straw and leather and souvenirs of Florentine craftsmanship. However, many centuries ago this was the place where the *carroccio* was kept, that is the war chariot bearing the symbols of the city that all the Italian communes had. In the event of war this ox-drawn chariot would lead the army to the sound of a bell that was installed on it. The bell of the Florentine chariot was called the 'Martinella', and the chariot was drawn by a pair of white oxen of the breed known as 'Chianina' – from the Val di Chiana close to Arezzo. Obviously, it was also adorned with the symbols of the city – lilies and lions – and with red hangings so that it would be clearly visible from a distance. The charioteers were known as 'grulli', a term that is used by Florentines, even today, to refer to people who are, we might say, pacifists in the battle of wits!

When the loggia is not overcrowded with stalls, it is possible to see on the pavement a marble disk that shows the point where the chariot was parked. In later times, this spot was used as the site of a humiliating punishment inflicted on those guilty of bankruptcy. In full view of the populace, their bottoms would be bared and bounced repeatedly up and down on the slab of marble. In Florence, the fountain of the *Porcellino* is famous for having the same role as the Trevi fountain in Rome: whoever throws in a coin can be sure of returning very soon to this beautiful city.

THE HOUSE OF DANTE ALIGHIERI

The so-called 'house of Dante' in Via Dante Alighieri is not actually the birthplace of the great poet, which was very probably demolished, since it was the practice at the time to destroy every trace of those 'ignoble beings' who, like Dante, were driven out of the city and condemned to perpetual exile. The house that we see now is simply a relatively recent reconstruction, purely imaginary in terms of both appearance and location which, although approximate, is far from precise. Nevertheless, Dante's house can't have been too far distant since he himself said that from his windows he could see the entrance to the Torre della Castagna where, while in office, he joined the other priors who governed the city. What is authentic is the little church of San Martino al Vescovo where Dante went to pray and perhaps also to sigh fondly in close proximity to the beautiful Beatrice Portinari, whom he loved and who attended mass in the same church.

THE TORRE DELLA ZECCA

In 1317 the city walls on the banks of the Arno terminated to the east in the tower that can still be seen today in Piazza Piave, tall and solitary almost like a ghost of the past. It is known as the tower 'of the Zecca' or the Mint, because for a while the Mint that produced the gold florins for the Florentine commune was housed here. Striking the coins required the

Fig. 34 - The Torre della Zecca

use of hammers that were raised by means of toothed wheels powered by the water flow, located in tunnels and chambers below the tower where there was plenty of water.

EIGHT CENTURIES OF BISCHERI

There is a term that even today, after many centuries, is frequently used in Florence, although generally the people who use it do not know exactly what it means. When someone does something stupid, or behaves in a way that is not intelligent, and especially when what has been done is not in the person's best interests, people will say 'You're a *bischero!*' This typically Florentine – and, in a broader sense, Tuscan – term has a slightly offensive but on the whole rather good-natured tone, since when they really want to offend the Florentines have a huge arsenal of much more effective terms and phrases at their disposal!

Going back to the Middle Ages we find that the Bischeri were a family of wealthy Florentine merchants, so that the phase 'You're a *bischero*' has to be understood literally in the sense of: 'you are a member of the Bischeri family', alluding to the fact that, many centuries ago, in a specific circumstance that family behaved in an unwise manner, so unwise that they suffered a vast financial loss. Therefore, in the Florentine phrase a 'bischero' is someone who behaves foolishly and against their own interests.

So, what did this family do that was so damaging to its interests? It seems that the Bischeri owned several plots of building land close to what is now Piazza del Duomo. The commune of Florence needed to buy these plots to erect buildings serving the city and, on several occasions, it offered the family considerable sums of money to sell them. But the Bischeri continued to refuse, in the conviction that the passage of time and the ever more pressing building requirements of the commune would push the value of the plots to the highest possible level. For a good while, things continued in this stalemate, with renewed offers met with fresh refusals, then suddenly something happened that tipped the scales in an unexpected manner. Tired of these constant refusals, the commune forcibly bought up the land in question through a compulsory purchase order and for an amount that was absolutely paltry compared to the previous offers.

Being a family of merchants, the Bischeri were anything but inexperienced in matters of business, and hence of looking after their own commercial interests, but in this case they tried to overreach themselves and by trying to be too smart they ended up with a result that was totally counter to their interests. From that day on the Florentines consider the Bischeri family of as an example of short-sighted foolishness, hence the family name became an eponym in the term 'bischero'.

A plaque for the Holy Year of 1300

The fact that today we are very familiar with many historical details about mediaeval Florence is in no small degree due to the Holy Year of 1300, known as that of 'universal pardon', that was proclaimed by Pope Boniface VIII.

In that Jubilee year a huge number of pilgrims, from Florence and all over Italy, travelled to Rome on pilgrimage to obtain remission of their sins. Among the most illustrious Florentines who went to Rome on that occasion was the historian Giovanni Villani (who has passed down to us so much information about Florence since ancient times in his *Chronicle*), the great poet Dante Alighieri, and Giotto who, on this occasion, was commissioned by the pope to execute two famous works, already mentioned in another chapter.

As Villani himself tells us, it was in Rome that he got the inspiration to write the history of Florence, a city that was the 'daughter of Rome'. As he wrote, 'and thus in the year 1300, having returned from Rome, I began to compile this book, in reverence to God and the blessed John, and in commendation of our city of Florence.'

An unknown Florentine, of whom we know only his first name Ugolino, was one of the many who set off with his wife on pilgrimage to Rome in that Holy Year. Unlike other pilgrims, however, Ugolino wished to leave to posterity a tangible sign of his journey to Rome. We have to admit that he succeeded perfectly in his intent, since even today, over seven centuries later, in the street where he lived there still exists a plaque, inscribed in Latin, that recalls his journey to Rome for the indulgence, concluding in Italian 'and Ugolino went there with his wife'. Anyone who should wish to see that ancient plaque has only to visit the street where Ugolino lived, in what was probably not a very wealthy district since the street was called Via della Fogna (Sewer Street). But take care because, although the street still exists, it changed its name a long time ago to Via Giovanni da Verrazzano.

THE PRANKS OF BUFFALMACCO

As in all categories of people, among artists too there have always been those who like to play pranks. In fourteenth-century Florence there was one artist in particular, who specialised mostly in tabernacles, but spent more time playing tricks on people than on painting. His name was Buffalmacco Buonamico. Such a strange and funny name makes one think of a character invented for a fairy tale. Instead, he really did exist although, evidently, he paid the price for his mania for playing pranks since it would seem that not one of his paintings has survived. There is actually another explanation for the total absence of his works, considering that as we said he was a painter of Madonnas and saints for the numerous tabernacles that were to be found at the time at almost every street corner. It stands to reason that such fragile constructions could not withstand the wear and weather of centuries. What have come down to us, however, are the tales of all the tricks he played on many Florentines of the time, which I suppose is just another way of acquiring the 'immortality' that he would otherwise not have had.

To give you an idea of Buffalmacco, let's take the episode of one of his neighbours. This poor woman, as well as cooking and doing housework all day long, was then also obliged by her husband to sit up until late at night weaving on the loom, and the continual beating of the shuttle on the frame disturbed the sleep of Buffalmacco, who lived next door. Tired of this situation, one morning the artist filled up a long cane with salt and, positioning himself at an open window, blew all the salt down the cane and into the soup that the woman was boiling on the fire. The woman's husband found the extremely salty soup uneatable, but above all he finally realised that he could not expect his wife to cook decently if she was half-asleep during the day. As a result, to Buffalmacco's great satisfaction, from that evening on the poor woman was able to rest at night like everyone else.

Unfortunately, among Buffalmacco's pranks, there was also one that ended in tragedy. During the May Day festivities in 1304, as was the custom companies and bands of youths would go through the city rejoicing and merrymaking. The people from south of the river – called *sanfrianini* after the district of Borgo San Friano (now San Frediano) – were famous for inventing the most amusing pastimes and spectacles, and they sent forth a proclamation to the whole city that 'whosoever desired news of the other world should come on 1st May upon the Carraia Bridge, and beside the Arno'. The Florentines were extremely curious about this spectacle, and they rushed in great numbers to see how the *sanfrianini* would represent the world beyond the grave. Buffalmacco, who had designed and organised the performance, wanted to recreate a representation of hell that was so realistic and frightful that it would give the shivers to everyone. This is how Villani describes the episode that ended so tragically,

and they erected upon the Arno a stage upon boats and vessels, and thereupon they made the similitude and figure of hell, with fires and other pains and sufferings, with men disguised as demons, horrible to behold, and others which had the appearance of naked souls, which seemed to be persons, and they were putting them to the said divers torments, with loud cries, and shrieks, and tumult, which seemed hateful and fearful to hear and to see.

Buffalmacco's imaginative flair proved to be truly exceptional on this occasion. Unfortunately the Carraia bridge, onto which an incredible number of people had crowded to view the spectacle, was made of timbers resting on masonry piers. What happened was that in several places the timbers caved in under the huge weight of the massive crowd and the bridge collapsed. Many people drowned in the Arno and many others perished as they fell onto the piers or onto the boats passing beneath the bridge.

Villani ended the chronicle of the tragedy with this reflection, 'So that the pastime from sport became earnest, and, as the proclamation had said, many by death went to learn news of the other world.'

Buffalmacco himself did not die in the disaster but, as Vasari in his *Lives* tells us,

He died at the age of seventy-eight, and being very poor and having done more spending than earning, by reason of being such in character, he was supported in his illness by the Company of the Misericordia in Santa Maria Nuova, the hospital of Florence; and

131

then, being dead, he was buried in the Ossa (for so they call a cloister, or rather cemetery, of the hospital), like the rest of the poor, in the year 1340.

THE PALAZZO DEL BARGELLO

At the beginning of the thirteenth century, the Council of Elders of the Florentine government used to meet in the Baptistery of San Giovanni, where all the new citizens of Florence were

Fig. 35 - The Palazzo del Bargello

Fig. 36 - Drawing showing the profile of Dante Alighieri taken from
Giotto's fresco of *Paradise* in the chapel of the Bargello

baptised as soon as they came into the world. It was in fact the largest church in the city and, in view of its octagonal form, was particularly well suited for meetings. But there was also another reason for preferring it to other venues: since it was dedicated to the patron saint of Florence, it was the most appropriate location for the council, with St John as the supreme symbol endorsing the freedom of the commune.

On the other hand, the Capitano del Popolo had his office – known as the 'Credenza' – in a very modest dwelling close to Santo Stefano al Ponte. A more appropriate premises had to be found for him, and a plot of land close to the Badia Fiorentina was duly selected. Here, on the corner between what are now Via del Proconsolo and Via Ghibellina, in 1256 the Palagio del Capitano was built, which only later came to be known as the 'Bargello'.

Installed next to the Capitano del Popolo was a notary who drew up the deliberations and composed the official letters in erudite language. In doing so, it often happened that he had to cancel or cross out words and phrases that were not written in the most eloquent manner and in the best form and style. It is from this constant need to cross out, or in Italian *cancellare*, that the term defining the office of *cancelliere*, or chancellor, derives.

In the Palazzo del Bargello, more specifically in the chapel of Santa Maria Maddalena (also known as the 'Cappella del Podestà'), a fascinating cycle of frescoes was discovered in the nineteenth century and attributed to Giotto, although the most recent scholarship attributes the frescoes only to the school of Giotto. For centuries the frescoes had been covered with plaster containing corrosive mortar that had greatly damaged them, and they were clumsily patched up, repainting the sections of corroded colour. A recent excellent restoration, carried out following the best practice for this specific type of painting, has succeeded in fairly decently saving what could be saved. The fresco of *Paradise* on the altar wall actually includes a portrait of Dante as a young man, identified in the figure in the group to the right, dressed in crimson. This portrait appears to be the one that is most faithful to the real features of the great poet, since he and Giotto were practically the same age – Giotto just one year younger – and also great friends. Another interesting curiosity is that one of the men who discovered the frescoes in the chapel was an English painter and Dante scholar called Seymour Kirkup. Kirkup was also in possession of a mask of the face of Dante Alighieri, traditionally believed to have been made from a mould taken from the corpse of the poet, which is now conserved in Palazzo Vecchio. This mask also plays a key role in Dan Brown's recent novel *Inferno*.

THE OSPEDALE DEGLI INNOCENTI

Overlooking Piazza Santissima Annunziata – on the left with one's back to the church – the beautiful loggia, adorned with medallions in glazed terracotta by Andrea della Robbia, is part of the ancient Ospedale degli Innocenti: another superb masterpiece by the famous and ingenious fifteenth-century architect Filippo Brunelleschi. In this case, 'Innocenti' does not refer to any alleged family that may have commissioned the hospital, since families with this surname appeared only later. Here, instead, the term refers to the innocent infants who were abandoned because their parents were unable, or unwilling, to take care of them. The opening of this special hospital – the first institution of its kind in Europe – was undoubtedly one of the greatest social achievements of Florence, and the merit for it goes largely to the ancient Silk Guild which, even more than other guilds, provided assistance by 'giving alms to poor men and women, helping the sick, finding husbands for young girls, assisting prisoners, women in childbirth, and other works of mercy'. So, in 1421, the Silk Guild entrusted to Brunelleschi the task of constructing this building for foundlings, or as they were called *gettatelli*, that is innocent babes literally 'cast aside' by parents 'who have deserted them against the laws of nature'. These unhappy little victims of sin, of shame, but more often than not, simply of poverty and misery, were to have a splendid home into which they could be welcomed like the most deserving of God's creatures. At one end of the fine classical portico, on the side of the building bordering with what is now Via della Colonna, there was a low window closed by a species of revolving wooden drum known as the *rota*, or wheel. The person wishing to abandon the baby would place it on the surface of the wheel and then give the drum a half-turn so that the infant was transferred to the inside of the edifice. Then she or he would pull a cord that rang a small bell inside the hospital to alert the staff to the presence of a baby in the *rota*, and would then quickly move off, as merciful hands within would rush to welcome the little new arrival.

As these very foundlings grew up and took their places within the city population, they gave rise to the spread of the surnames typical of those who had been raised as foundlings and had been given a surname by the staff of the hospital. These are eloquent and touching names such as Innocenti, Degli Innocenti, Degli Esposti, Diotisalvi, Diotallevi, and similar.

THE FLORINS 'WALLED INTO' THE CONVENT OF SAN MARCO

The beautiful church and adjacent convent of San Marco in the square of the same name belong to the Dominican friars., Following the demolition of the pre-existing mediaeval convent, the complex was built around the middle of the fifteenth century by Michelozzo, and it reveals the inspiration of Brunelleschi, especially in two light-filled cloisters. As Michelozzo gradually completed the structural elements of the convent, one of the friars, Fra Giovanni da Fiesole – universally famous under the better-known name of Beato Angelico – would set himself to painting on the still fresh plaster. It is indeed the frescoes and paintings by him that are conserved here that have contributed to making this museum and church famous all over the world.

Beato Angelico was also an illuminator and has even been defined – perhaps with little artistic consideration – as the precursor of the comic strip. This is because of the scrolls with writing on them that he used to paint near his figures, often close to the mouth, giving the impression that the people represented pronounced those words, as in a comic. The truth is that Beato Angelico was a great artist who succeeded in encapsulating the turning-point between a still late-Gothic vision of painting and a three-dimensional Renaissance vision of great pictorial effect. Beato Angelico's conviction was that 'everything on this earth is willed by God and in Him everything is resolved'. This transpires in all his works, especially in the panel called the *Tabernacle of the Linaioli* and the frescoes in the Chapter House, the Refectory, the friars' cells and the large cloister. We can understand all this much better if we bear in mind that Beato Angelico usually painted his works kneeling, except when he was required to do otherwise by the particular position of the scenes to be painted. In this way, not only did he give his paintings the value of prayers, but further strengthened this aspect by actually reciting prayers as he painted, in the conviction that God alone could guide his hand.

It seems unbelievable, but if today we can admire these magnificent works of art, we owe it to the prickly conscience of a powerful lord who, at a certain point of his life, began to realise that he had probably become too rich and in a not entirely honest manner. 25 October 1436, the feast of the Annunciation, was the day planned for the consecration of the Cathedral of Florence which had finally been completed, albeit without the lantern. To celebrate this ceremony Pope Eugene IV came to Florence, where he was received with all honours by the Lord of Florence, Cosimo I de' Medici. However, Cosimo had been troubled for some time by doubts about the fate of his soul, and his conscience was not clear, knowing how unjustly he had piled up riches for himself to the detriment both of his own people and of others. So, he decided to confide in the pope and ask him in what way he could relieve his conscience of this weight. Clearly, a mere confession would not suffice: the moral law called for the return of ill-gotten gains, although in his case this would have been extremely difficult considering the number of injured parties involved!

The penance that the pope gave Cosimo was to wall up 10,000 gold florins in the convent of San Marco. But these florins were not to be literally walled up, in the sense of concealed within the walls, but rather in the sense of using the money to rebuild the old convent. Cosimo therefore gave precise instructions that, cost what it might, everything necessary should be done to make San Marco the finest convent in the world. This is why Michelozzo was able to build this magnificent complex which, as it turned

Fig. 37 - Stone set into the pavement of Piazza della Signoria marking the spot where Girolamo Savonarola was hanged and burned at the stake

out, cost Cosimo I much more than ten thousand florins. Indeed, the superb construction 'for the relief of his soul' in the end cost him the tidy sum of 40,000 gold florins!

THE BELL THAT WAS 'BANISHED'

In the cloister of St Antoninus in this same convent of San Marco, up to a short time ago there was a very large bell. It was attached to a species of gantry set on the ground, and obstructed the passage of visitors. It appeared to be – and indeed it was – waiting to be put in its rightful place, or rather, hoping to be replaced in its belfry. Poor bell! After so many vicissitudes, it wanted to go back to the place that it had occupied for so many years. It was indeed the very bell that had pealed out so often from the top of the belltower of San Marco in the times of Girolamo

138

Savonarola and the Medici. But it was never to be replaced there, and was ultimately moved to its final location in the Chapter House of the adjacent Museum of San Marco. This unfortunate bell even has a mournful name: *Piagnona*, or 'weeper'.

'Piagnoni', or weepers, was also the name given to the followers of Girolamo Savonarola, the feisty friar who was an outspoken opponent of the luxurious lifestyle embodied in the powerful Medici family that governed Florence. Savonarola was an implacable moral scourge, advocating a return to piety and contempt for earthly desires. His adversaries, that is the faction favourable to the Medici, called themselves 'Palleschi', deriving from the *palle*, or balls, on the Medici coat of arms. Clashes, even violent, between the two factions were the order of the day, and often ended in injuries. One day, during one such riot, Savonarola found himself at risk of his life and had to take refuge in the convent of San Marco, which was immediately besieged by the angry mob. To summon help from Savonarola's supporters, the friars set the great convent bell ringing uninterruptedly – the same bell that was later named *Piagnona* – this alarm successfully scattered the rioters and the friar's life was saved on this occasion.

However, Savonarola's inflexibility eventually brought him into conflict even with the pope, after which things really began to look bad for him: he was arrested, tried, and condemned to death by hanging and then being burned at the stake.

The public execution took place in Piazza della Signoria on 23 May 1498, when Savonarola was put to death along with two of his fellow friars who had supported him. The exact point where the execution took place is marked by a round slab of porphyry with an inscription in bronze set into the pavement of the square close to Palazzo Vecchio.

But this story did not end with the death of Savonarola. There is an epilogue that deserves to be recalled.

Deprived of their leader, the *Piagnoni* had by now disbanded. But there was still a guilty party to be judged and condemned: that accursed bell which by pealing uninterruptedly had once saved the friar's life and which from that day on was referred to by the Palleschi as *Piagnona*.

It seems ridiculous to attribute guilt to an inanimate object such as a bell when, if anything, it should have been attributed to the people who rang it. But that was the mentality of the time, the same mentality that led to the demolition of the houses belonging to those who had been exiled from the city. While this species of *damnatio memoriae* may seem incomprehensible to us, for our ancestors it was not only logical but taken for granted.

And so that bell, which from the belfry of San Marco had dared to summon the *Piagnoni* to gather in defence of Savonarola, was tried and sentenced to be removed from the belltower and, to ensure that its peal would never again be heard, it was in effect banished to the church of San Salvatore al Monte (close to Piazzale Michelangelo) and its place in the belfry was taken by another bell. When, a long time later, the bell was deemed to have served its sentence through a sufficient period of banishment, it was permitted to return to the convent of San Marco, not to its place of honour in the belfry, but on the ground in the cloister where it remained from the Renaissance almost up to the end of the last century.

DONATELLO'S SATISFACTION

Donatello is considered the greatest Florentine sculptor of the fifteenth century. One of the stories told about him recounts that in 1415, when he had just finished sculpting the superb statue of *St John the Evangelist* – now in the Museo dell'Opera del Duomo – Donatello was so satisfied with it that he gave the statue a light blow with the hammer and said to it 'Speak!'

It was apparently not unusual for the artists of the past to react in this way. It seems that one day Michelangelo, upon seeing another statue by Donatello, this time the *St George* that is now in the Bargello museum, exclaimed with admiration 'Walk!' What could be higher praise?

OSSA EQUI

While the emperor Charles V was besieging Florence in 1539, a cannon shot from the imperial army fell in Piazza dei Giudici, killing the horse of the Venetian ambassador Carlo Capello. The horse was buried in a tomb in the very same square, marked by a plaque on the wall of the lungarno celebrating the memory of his equine companion and bearing the Latin inscription: *Ossa equi Caroli Capelli Legati Veneti* (bones of the horse of the Venetian legate Carlo Capello).

THE PERFECTION OF A BRIDGE

Although since ancient times the Florentines have been perfectly capable of pronouncing the word 'Trinità' when referring to the three persons of God, when they refer to the church of Santa Trinita or to the bridge that was named after that church, they shift the accent from the final syllable 'à' to the first syllable 'tri'. And so, let us too respect this deformation originating from the *vox populi* and pronounce this name in the Florentine manner, probably attributable to the Latin derivation.

Ponte Santa Trinita has been called the most beautiful bridge in the world, and precisely on account of its beauty was at length attributed to the great Michelangelo. It is instead extremely probable that the bridge was designed by Bartolomeo Ammannati, who adopted in its curvatures the so-called 'catenary curve' that Michelangelo used in the Medici Chapels of San Lorenzo,

Fig. 38 - View of Ponte Santa Trinita, clearly showing
the catenary curve conceived by Michelangelo

which was probably the reason for the initial error of attribution to Michelangelo. There are, however, certain art historians that sustain a different hypothesis: namely that the bridge was designed by Michelangelo while Ammannati was in charge of its construction. Nevertheless, although this would suggest that the true paternity of the bridge seems destined to remain a mystery, there are valid reasons for not seeing it as such. Not only does the most recent art history scholarship attribute it officially to Bartolomeo Ammannati, but other considerations also support this attribution.

One of the reasons why the bridge is so beautiful is that the piers are not set at equal distances from each other, and as a result the curves of the arches are not identical either. So, Ammannati must have studied the currents of the Arno, placing the piers in the best possible positions, and designing them in the form of a spur, almost like the prow of a ship. The three flattened ellipses

142

of the arches were then constructed on these piers, with all points studied and calibrated to such a degree of precision that, were it not for the parapet, the structure would appear reduced to an absolute minimum. Moreover, the arch could not have been simply taken from a prefabricated model, since it has clearly been studied in such a way as to perfectly sustain the weight. Finally, there is an elasticity and tension of the lines that is not characteristic of Michelangelo. We may therefore conclude that, even if the initial idea was Michelangelo's, the rest is undoubtedly the work of Ammannati.

The Ponte Santa Trinita that we see today is not the original, which was blown up by German mines during the Second World War; nevertheless, the bridge that we can all admire now downstream of Ponte Vecchio is a perfect replica.

Before proceeding to the rebuilding of this bridge in the late 1950s, since the Florence City Council intended to rebuild it identical, it decided to have the original design checked by the best-qualified modern engineers and architects to see whether anything in the curvature or other structural elements ought to be altered or adjusted to ensure greater stability. Based on the meticulous study of photographs of the destroyed bridge, the sixteenth-century design was translated into technical drawings and, substantially, analysed from every possible angle, with every detail being subjected to the most stringent examination in line with the state of the art of construction science. The outcome of this exacting analysis was that not a single curve or structural element proved to come anything short of perfect, and this very perfection was what enabled the destroyed bridge to be rebuilt exactly identical to the original. This should also make us pause to render just merit, not only to Ammannati, but to all the great architects of the past, who created their daring works more on the strength of their personal genius and extensive experience than on scientific knowledge.

Fig. 39 - *Judith and Holofernes*, by Donatello

Would-be Tour Guides

I should like to end this chapter dedicated to so many interesting titbits by telling the amusing story of an episode that took place many years ago in Piazza della Signoria during a guided tour. This was the period immediately following the Second World War. Today an episode of this kind could not take place, but in those days the people proposing themselves as tour guides were not always qualified. Indeed, it happened quite often that people who were anything but well-informed on artistic matters would improvise as tour guides (known as *ciceroni*) in order to earn a bit of money.

This anecdote, which is well-known especially among the 'over 65' Florentine seniors, recounts that a young lad, evidently a self-styled tour guide, was taking a group of tourists on a tour of the statues in Piazza della Signoria. When they reached Donatello's statue of *Judith and Holofernes* the guide explained: 'This, ladies and gentlemen, is Judith, cutting off the head of Holofernes; it is a work by the great Donatello and symbolises justice!' After the usual admiring comments, the small group moved on to other statues, arriving finally at Benvenuto Cellini's *Perseus*, at which the young guide exclaimed: 'Here we are. You see? This statue too represents justice, and it was made by no less than the great Cellini!' Since the youth had not mentioned who the figures shown in the statue were, either because he had forgotten or because he didn't know, some of the tourists asked him about it. But the poor guide, taken unawares, found himself unable to recall the name of either Perseus or the Medusa. He tried to take a covert look at his guide book for the answer, but in his confusion failed to find it. So, in order not to prolong too much the embarrassing silence, he blurted out the first thing that came into his head: 'That, em … that is Holofernes cutting off the head of Judith!' Obviously, the tourists who had just seen Donatello's statue could not accept such a reply, and one of them began to protest loudly. Despite

145

having realised – too late – that he had made a colossal blunder, the would-be guide promptly – and in a very Florentine manner – retorted: 'My dear sir, *la un lo sa che a Firenze, icché gli è fatto l'è reso?*' (literally: don't you know that in Florence what you give – for better or worse – is what you get?).

THE FLORENTINES WHO DISCOVERED AMERICA

Everyone knows that it was Christopher Columbus who discovered America. However, with all due respect for the great explorer from Genoa, he actually believed that he had reached India, which is why the Native Americans are still to this day known incorrectly as Red Indians, and it was Columbus himself who called them that because he believed them to be inhabitants of India.

It was, in fact, another great navigator – the Florentine Amerigo Vespucci – who realised Columbus's mistake: that was not India, but a new continent which was then called America after Vespucci. But it was not Amerigo himself who named the new continent discovered by Columbus 'America'. He simply observed that these were new lands, hitherto unknown, and not India. Therefore, Vespucci never thought – as some maintain – of usurping the fame of Columbus, but openly gave him the credit for having discovered the New World. It was others – including the German cartographer and humanist Martin Waldseemüller – who recognised the merit of the Florentine navigator by calling the new continent America, quite unbeknownst to Vespucci. Vespucci was a contemporary of Columbus, and had already been in Seville for a year when Columbus set sail from Palos with his caravels.

Fig. 40 - Portrait of Amerigo Vespucci (anonymous)

The Vespucci family were part of the ancient Florentine nobility and lived in a mansion in Borgo Ognissanti, not far from the church of Ognissanti that still stands in the same street, in which you can still see, on the right, an altar characterised by the *vespe*, or wasps of the family. The coat of arms of the Vespucci in fact had a red field, with an oblique blue band bearing seven golden wasps, so that the name clearly derives from the wasps, or *vespe*. A painting of the *Madonna of Mercy* on the altar of this chapel shows members of the Vespucci family, although it is not clear whether Amerigo is the young boy close to the Madonna, or the slightly older youth shown in the *Lamentation* beneath. The date of Amerigo's birth is not certain: in the 'book of ages' it is recorded as March 1452, but in the 'book of the baptised' as March 1454.

In some lines written by Vespucci – although not all scholars are agreed about their authenticity – he explains the reasons which made him stop being a merchant and become a navigator: 'I decided to leave off the mercantile career, and set upon entering one that would be more stable and praiseworthy. I was disposed to see some of the world and its wonders.' Or again, 'We left from the port of Cadiz and we took our way for the Great Gulf of the Ocean Sea, on which voyage we took 17 months, discovering a great deal of mainland, and an infinite number of islands, most of them inhabited'.

Vespucci described his voyages and discoveries in the greatest detail: he was so excited that he found it hard to sleep 'very often I lost the night's sleep'. He was an expert in the use of the sailing instruments, such as the quadrant and the astrolabe, and he navigated at length, exploring the lands, naming them and drawing them meticulously: Mexico, Honduras, Nicaragua, Costa Rica, Columbia, Venezuela, Brazil, Uruguay and Patagonia, as far as the gulf that he called 'San Lorenzo' possibly in memory of Lorenzo de' Medici.

The names that he gave to the individual places that he discovered – bays, gulfs, and coasts – referred to the saint of the day in which the discovery took place. For instance, the 'Bay of All Saints' discovered on 1 November, All Saints' Day, which gave him particularly great joy, considering that his parish in Florence was Ognissanti! Among the many others, we can also mention the Bay of Kings, discovered on 6 January, the Feast of the Epiphany, and hence of the Magi so dear to his childhood memories. Instead, his reason for the naming of Venezuela (or little Venice), was that the houses built on the sea reminded him of Venice.

It was precisely by sailing and making constant cartographic surveys along these coasts that Vespucci realised that these lands formed the vertex of a vast triangle which, taken as whole, could be none other than an immense continent. Amerigo Vespucci also made other voyages – although the actual number is still controversial – by virtue of which, and of the rich results he brought home, he was nominated *Piloto mayor*, or Master Navigator, by Queen Joanna of Castille. As a good Florentine and a good Christian, he never failed to combine practical utility with respect for God. Indeed he wrote,

This journey, which I now see is dangerous as to the liberty of this human life of ours. Nevertheless, I undertake it with a sincere heart to serve God and the world. And if God will act through me, He will give me virtue, just as I am prepared for every wish of His, so that He may grant me the eternal repose of my soul.

Amerigo conserved the rank of *Piloto mayor*, and of supreme regulator of Atlantic cartography, up to his death, which took place in Seville at just 58 years of age.

Nor can we overlook another great navigator that the city of Florence – despite being anything but maritime – has given to the world: Giovanni da Verrazzano. One of the numerous plaques that adorn the ancient mansions of illustrious Florentines can be found on an old house in Via Giovanni da Verrazzano in the district of Santa Croce. This is where the family of this other great Florentine navigator lived.

Giovanni was born in Florence around 1485, he too into an ancient family which originally came from the Val di Greve where it owned the ancestral Castle of Verrazzano. Giovanni spent his youth between the castle of his forbears and the house in Florence, and the noble coat of arms was for him almost a portent of his life as a navigator: in fact, the crest showed a red eight-pointed star on a gold and silver field, which strangely enough very closely resembled a compass rose!

After an excellent humanist education, and having visited distant lands such as Syria and Egypt to learn about trade, Giovanni became enthralled by the accounts of the fantastic voyages made by Columbus, with their tales of exotic peoples and animals and luxuriant vegetation, all things that had never been seen before. The greatest explorers of the time were looking for the famous 'northwest passage' through these new lands, which would then allow the trade routes to reach Cathay (China).

Giovanni is recorded as having been in Portugal in 1517, from where he followed or accompanied Ferdinand Magellan to Spain on the eve of the great circumnavigation. His presence in France in 1522 is also indisputably recorded. It seems that he set off on his first voyage from France with a fleet of four ships in December 1524, but was taken over by a storm. He then set out again from Madeira around the middle of January with a single caravel and a crew of around fifty. Verrazzano's objective was to observe and accurately survey the coastline to discover any possible passages. Since he was headed further north from the lands that had already been explored, these coasts were all yet to be discovered. Giovanni, good Florentine that he was, marked and named all the elements of coastline that he came across with names that were typically Florentine, or at least Tuscan, such as Annunziata, Careggi, Monte Morello, San Gallo, Impruneta, Livorno, etc.

One day he explored a beautiful bay, which he described in detail in a letter reporting to the King of France:

so we took the small boat and sailed up this river to the land, which we found densely populated, the people being almost the same as the others. They were dressed in birds' feathers of various colours. They came towards us joyfully, with great cries of admiration, and showing us the safest place to land the boat. We went up the river for about half a league, where we found that it widened into a beautiful lake with a circumference of about 9 leagues, where about thirty of their boats, crowded with people were sailing back and forth from one side to the other to come to see us.

Giovanni da Verrazzano named this bay 'Santa Margherita' in honour of the king's sister. Subsequently its name was changed twice, the second time by the English who gave it the name it still bears: none other than New York!

Unfortunately, Giovanni came to a sticky end. He was accustomed to meeting indigenous people who were always kind and welcoming, enthusiastic about the trinkets that the sailors gave them, such as coloured beads, bells and mirrors. However, one day Giovanni landed on an island, convinced that he would meet the usual well-disposed natives. But the people that crowded around him behaved very differently, disdaining every form of trinket that was offered to them. Even the mirrors – that had driven all the other natives they had met so far crazy with joy – had no effect at all on them. Why such strange behaviour? Evidently the natives of that small island had very different tastes. The fact is that they were cannibals, and indeed they ate poor Giovanni and almost all his companions. This happened in the year 1528.

Michelangelo Buonarroti

We have left to the last – albeit certainly not least in terms of importance – several chapters devoted to the life and genius of Michelangelo. He was undoubtedly one of the greatest Florentines of all time, and his long life as a man and an artist is packed with anecdotes and curiosities.

Fig. 41 - Anonymous drawing showing Michelangelo Buonarroti

MEDICI DUOS: THE TWO GIULIANOS
AND THE TWO 'MAGNIFICENT' LORENZOS

While he was in Florence, Giovanni de' Medici – who later became pope as Leo X – decided to complete the church of San Lorenzo in the square of the same name, commissioning the works from Michelangelo. The great artist was to provide a facade for the church, although he was prevented from doing so by political intrigues and the envy of his colleagues. He was also asked to design – symmetrical to the Old Sacristy containing the tombs of Giovanni di Bicci and of Cosimo's sons Giovanni and Piero – the New Sacristy for the tombs of the more important Lorenzo and Giuliano, who were involved in the Pazzi Conspiracy, and for those of the new generation who were still alive, of whom the pope and Giulio were the oldest.

However, as fate would have it, to die first it was the younger members of the family, Giuliano, Duke of Nemours, and Lorenzo, Duke of Urbino, respectively son and grandson of Lorenzo the Magnificent. As a result, Michelangelo had to immediately set to work on their sepulchres, carving what was to become the most solemn and heartbreaking monument of Florentine art, ingeniously overturning the previous conception of the sarcophagus as showing the deceased person in the composed serenity of death. Michelangelo instead placed upon the tombs figures that were larger than life, in impressive idealisations with tormented plays of light and shade. Indeed, upon entering the New Sacristy of San Lorenzo, one is immediately struck by the beauty of the figures representing *Night* and *Day*, and *Dusk* and *Dawn*. In actual fact, these statues do not symbolise the times of the day, as it might seem, but rather the times of human life from youth to age, in an unfurling of time the substance of which is ambiguous, dominated on the one hand by mortal destiny and on the other by eternity.

But once the stunned wonder of the first impression passes, and one begins to observe this extraordinary sculptural complex in greater detail, anyone without an expert knowledge of Florentine history might be struck by a doubt upon noticing something strange. The fact is that – apart from the title of 'Duke' following the name – the figures buried in the sacristy are: Giuliano de' Medici and Lorenzo de' Medici known as 'the Magnificent', *and* Giuliano de' Medici and Lorenzo de' Medici known as 'the Magnificent'! This is not a mistake. Buried here there are indeed two Giulianos and two Lorenzos, and both the Lorenzos were known as the 'Magnificent', even though if truth be told one deserved this title much more than the other.

The allegorical figures of *Night* and *Day* recline upon the lid of the sarcophagus of Giuliano de' Medici, Duke of Nemours, brother of the Giovanni who became Pope Leo X and son of the great Lorenzo who truly deserved to be called 'the Magnificent'. The Duke died of tuberculosis in 1516 at the age of 37.

Dusk and *Dawn* are the recumbent figures on the sarcophagus of Lorenzo de' Medici, Duke of Urbino, who was also, somewhat improperly, known as the 'Magnificent'. He was the nephew of Giuliano, Duke of Nemours and Pope Leo X, and grandson of the Lorenzo rightly dubbed 'the Magnificent'. The Duke of Urbino died at the age of just 26 of intestinal tuberculosis.

By contrast, also in the New Sacristy is a simple tomb, devoid of ornament and almost anonymous, that houses the remains of the more famous Giuliano who was killed in the Pazzi Conspiracy, and his brother Lorenzo, the true Magnificent and Lord of Florence. What is the reason for this marked contrast which seems so unjust in penalising the more important figures to the advantage of the less important? The same political events, court intrigues and fierce rivalries of his fellow artists that prevented Michelangelo from executing the facade of San Lorenzo also prevented him from completing the other tombs in the New Sacristy. This is why we cannot admire who knows what other masterpieces by Michelangelo on this bare tomb, upon which there is nevertheless his beautiful marble *Madonna and Child*. Set on either side of the *Madonna* are statues of the two medical saints Cosmas and Damian, who were the patrons of the Medici, executed respectively by two artists who were contemporaries of Michelangelo, respectively Giovanni Angelo da Montorsoli and Raffaello da Montelupo. And so, quarrels and intrigues deprived two of the most famous Medici of a more fitting funeral monument.

The conception of that particular catenary curve of Michelangelo's that we mentioned in relation to the bridge of Santa Trinita is clearly visible in the lids of the two sarcophagi with the figures of *Night* and *Day*, *Dusk* and *Dawn*. As regards the statues above these, showing the Duke of Nemours and the Duke of Urbino, there is a story that tells how Michelangelo was working on these two statues, idealising their faces without any concern about their resemblance to the true features. When someone pointed this out to him, Michelangelo quickly rebuffed: 'What does it matter? In future centuries no one will recall the features of the two Medici in any way other than how I have sculpted them!'

MICHELANGELO THE FORGER

Michelangelo's contemporaries were amazed by the speed with which he sculpted his magnificent works, and many of his fellow sculptors were very envious of this gift of his. An envy which, as we have seen, prevented Michelangelo from realising certain other masterpieces in Florence. When people asked him what was his secret for creating such beautiful statues, and so quickly, from huge and formless blocks of marble, he would reply: 'It's simple, the statue is already there inside the stone, all you have to do is remove all the extra stone around it with hammer and chisel, and in this way free the figure that's inside!'

Michelangelo's skill as a sculptor became evident from a very tender age. He was little more than twenty when a Florentine antiquarian asked him to sculpt a *Sleeping Cupid* in the classical style. At that time Michelangelo was anything but rich and, to earn a few florins, was very willing even to do works that he could not infuse with his own great personality. He naively agreed to produce this 'classical' statue, not realising the obscure purpose for which the astute and dishonest antiquarian had requested such a work. He duly executed the *Sleeping Cupid* in antique classical style, making such a good job of it that the antiques dealer had no difficulty at all in selling it as an authentic antiquity at a very high price. As ill-luck would have it, the purchaser who was cheated by the statue was that same Cardinal Riario who, 18 years before, had risked being hanged by Lorenzo de' Medici for his part in the Pazzi Conspiracy that cost Giuliano's life. The cardinal admired this 'classical antique' so much that, as soon as he returned to Rome, he put it in the place of honour in his personal gallery of works of art, of which he was a great lover and an erudite expert.

However, misfortunes never come singly, and indeed it turned out that a friend of Michelangelo's – although it is more probable that it was an envious colleague – had happened to turn up in Michelangelo's workshop precisely when he was carving the *Sleeping Cupid*. Some time later this person – friend or envious fellow artist as he was – went to Rome and, being an acquaintance of Cardinal Riario, was invited to visit his art collection. You can imagine his surprise when, among so many pieces of inestimable value, he spotted the *Cupid* which he had accidentally seen Michelangelo working on. He was even more surprised when the cardinal pointed out this piece to him as the 'rarest' of his collection.

We shall never know the identity of this person who, visiting the cardinal's gallery, discovered the forgery made by Michelangelo, nor do we know how he communicated it to Riario. Some say that, when the cardinal told him that it was a classical antiquity, the visitor, being fully aware of how things really stood, burst out laughing, and was then obviously constrained to explain why. If this were the case, then the revelation of the forgery would not have been spurred by envy, but by chance, due to accidental and contingent circumstances, and there would have been no malicious intention towards Michelangelo.

Others instead maintain that this person was a sculptor who knew Michelangelo well and was evidently jealous of the great skill of his more eminent fellow artist, a skill such as to deceive even a great expert such as Riario into believing that the piece was authentic. He wanted to put in a bad light, if not Michelangelo's art, then at least his moral rectitude, revealing maliciously to the cardinal that the piece had to be a forgery, since he had seen it being made by Buonarroti with his own eyes.

We shall never know exactly how things went, but the upshot was that, as soon as Riario knew that the work was a forgery, he hit the ceiling for having been duped, taking it out on Michelangelo as the author of the work, regardless of the fact that the real trickster was the dishonest antiquarian who had sold him the statue passing it off as antique. Being openly accused of being a forger, Buonarroti went through a tough time and seriously risked a public trial. We can only imagine what the consequences would have been in the case that the artist had been condemned. Luckily Lorenzo de' Medici – the one who was later Duke of Urbino – advised Michelangelo to go immediately to Rome to see Riario and explain his position, and in this way forestall the trial. He also gave him a letter of recommendation to give to the cardinal, in which Lorenzo himself stood surety for the honesty and rectitude of Michelangelo, asserting that the responsibility for the forgery lay elsewhere.

Michelangelo immediately set off for Rome. This was June 1496, and it was the first time that the artist saw the city. Fortunately, although not without some difficulty, he succeeded in convincing the cardinal of his complete good faith. I imagine the reader's curiosity would want to know what happened to the fraudulent antiques dealer, but unfortunately the chronicles of this episode say nothing about it.

DAVID'S NOSE

The tourists who visit the Galleria dell'Accademia to admire the original of Michelangelo's statue of *David* will certainly not pause to observe with particular interest the nose of the biblical figure portrayed in this great masterpiece. However, if they happened to be aware of an event that really occurred, but that few people know about, they would be sure to look at this nose with curious attention.

Here we are, back in Florence in 1504 in the workshop of Michelangelo, where he has just completed one of his most famous sculptures, namely the celebrated *David*. On this occasion, the most eminent authorities of the Florentine Republic came to view this great statue – over four metres high, that they had commissioned to set it up in Piazza della Signoria in front of Palazzo Vecchio as a symbol to the world of the justice and liberty of the city. Among the dignitaries present who were complimenting the sculptor on the beauty of this new masterpiece of his, there was also the gonfalonier Piero Soderini, who was also a patron of the arts.

Possibly because he wanted to be noticed or perhaps to show everyone that he was an expert in artistic matters, Piero Soderini addressed himself to Michelangelo, saying, 'Yes, I absolutely agree, the *David* is magnificent; personally, however, I find that the nose is not well proportioned, and if with a few skilful chips of the chisel it could be made smaller, its artistic merit would be greatly enhanced'.

Michelangelo – who was well known for being very proud and touchy – would have liked to reply rudely to the arrogant gonfalonier, but given Soderini's political importance he checked himself so as not to spoil his relations with the Florentine government. On the other hand, nor did he wish to alter even the slightest detail of the statue that he considered perfect. With a stroke of genius worthy of his extraordinary character, he excogitated a solution that would at once save the nose of his masterpiece and at the same time make fun of the gonfalonier who had criticised it. The ingenuity of Michelangelo's solution lay in the fact that it did not entail the risk of any unpleasant consequence, since neither Piero Soderini nor the other dignitaries would notice it.

Pretending to agree to what had been suggested to him, the artist took a ladder and leaned it against the statue, then he picked a hammer off the ground with his right hand and a chisel with his left. But in taking the chisel off the ground, without anyone noticing he also picked up a handful of the marble dust and small chips that were lying all around the foot of the statue. Michelangelo then climbed up the ladder and drawing close to the nose of the sculpture began to strike the chisel with the hammer in full view of the city authorities. In actual fact, he was only pretending to strike the statue; keeping his left hand over David's nose, he took great care that the point of the chisel –

160

hidden by his hand, never actually touched the marble. To conceal his subterfuge and make his action more credible, as he struck the chisel with the hammer, he opened his left hand every so often to let fall some of the marble chips and dust that he had picked up. In this way he managed to convince everyone that he was really chiselling the nose of the statue. After a few minutes he came down the ladder and moved it away. Then he turned to the gonfalonier asking, 'How does it seem now?' Piero Soderini, who had been completely taken in by Michelangelo's ruse and had no idea that David's nose was exactly the same as before, exclaimed with an expression of proud satisfaction, 'Ah, you see I was right? Now, it really is perfect!'

DETAILS AND CURIOSITIES ABOUT THE 'DAVID'

Michelangelo's *David* is 5.17 metres high, complete with base, and was carved from a block of marble that was an archaeological ruin, apparently a large fragment of the architrave of an ancient building, possibly a temple, dating to the time of Imperial Rome. There is a curious anecdote about this piece of marble too. Before Michelangelo, various sculptors had attempted to carve this enormous block to produce a statue, but had given up the attempt because they claimed that it broke too easily, being old and full of cracks and veins. Michelangelo then decided to challenge the previous sculptors, saying, 'Let me see whether or not it really is possible to bring forth a statue from this old piece of marble!' He started work on it in 1501 to 'extract' his *David*, working on it more or less assiduously for three years up to 1504. As soon as it was finished, the statue was placed in Piazza della Signoria in front of Palazzo Vecchio, where it remained up to 1873.

In line with Michelangelo's Renaissance vision, David had to be naked like the ancient Greek *kouroi*, without

Fig. 42- Detail of Michelangelo's *David*

armour or breastplate: a symbol of justice and liberty. In fact, he vanquished his enemies not so much by weapons as by *virtus*, namely intelligence and inner strength. The statue is colossal because, standing in the Piazza, it had to be seen from a distance. In addition, the physical grandeur was also conceived as a symbol of moral grandeur.

In 1873 it was decided to remove the statue from the Piazza to prevent possible damage from the elements, and so it was transferred to the Galleria dell'Accademia in Via Ricasoli. Here the *David* is certainly well protected, but at the same time it is impossible to appreciate it to the full in view of its size. A marble replica was set up in Piazza della Signoria in its place. Another copy, in bronze, stands in a dominant position in Piazzale Michelangelo, overlooking Florence.

MICHELANGELO'S WAGER

On the facade of Palazzo Vecchio, almost behind the sculptural group of *Hercules and Cacus* by Baccio Bandinelli, close to the corner of the building towards Via della Ninna, there is a flat stone in the wall bearing the head of a man evidently made using a hammer and chisel, carved almost like a scratched graffito, although with a slightly deeper groove.

This graffito head can easily escape the attention of tourists passing through Piazza della Signoria; unless you go to look for it specifically, it is hard to make out on the grey stone walls of what is undoubtedly one of the most beautiful palaces in the world.

An anecdote that enjoys widespread popular credence tells that this head was carved by Michelangelo for a wager. The story goes that some of the artist's friends challenged him to carve the portrait of one of them in the stone while holding his hands behind his back. Michelangelo accepted the challenge and made this head with hammer and chisel without being able to see what he was doing, and in the very uncomfortable position of holding his hands behind his back to boot!' The story doesn't tell us whether or not Michelangelo won his wager, and therefore whether the figure reproduced resembled the original or not. There is no doubt, however, that the head is well done, vigorous and characteristic, and is by consensus agreed to be by the hand of the supreme artist. There is also another story about this head, albeit less credible, according to which Michelangelo happened to be in this place while the sorry cortege accompanying a condemned man to the gallows passed through the Piazza. Michelangelo was struck and moved to pity by this sad spectacle, and decided to rapidly sketch the face of the convict in the stone.

Fig. 43 - The graffito head on a stone in the wall of Palazzo Vecchio, attributed to Michelangelo

THE MILITARY GENIUS OF AN ARTIST WHO BELIEVED THAT MATTRESSES ARE NOT JUST FOR SLEEPING ON

Following the last bloodless banishment of the Medici from Florence, from June 1527 the banner of the liberty of the resurrected Florentine Republic fluttered once again from Palazzo Vecchio. At this time, Florence was isolated and helpless. Its political situation became increasingly difficult, despite the fact that, in the attempt to give the popular government greater stability, the gonfalonier of the Republic sought to come to an agreement with Pope Clement VII. However, Clement was a Medici – the nephew of Lorenzo the Magnificent – and as such was obviously rooting for the return to Florence of a government under the aegis of his own family. Pope Clement clearly displayed his intentions when he met the emperor Charles V in Barcelona in 1529, rapidly

164

reaching an agreement with him that effectively tolled the death knell on the popular Republic of Florence.

In the name of the emperor, Andrea Doria responded curtly to the Florentine ambassadors who sought to negotiate: 'You come too late and at a bad time!' And the pope gave no better response to the Florentine embassies. 'As much dominion and liberty as you wish, but as for popular government, not a chance: it has shown itself to be sectarian and lawless, and so it must return to the Medici!'

What could Florence hope for in attempting to stand up to the two greatest authorities and powers of the world, which were in perfect agreement about supressing that republic still so attached to its glorious civic traditions at a time when the great blocs were increasingly consolidated? Florence began to understand that the banner of its independence – red with white cross – would not be flying for much longer from the tall tower of Palazzo Vecchio. When the council met in the ancient palace the question was posed dramatically: what could be done in such conditions of unequal struggle? 'Resist!' replied the Florentines, and if necessary, even die for liberty!

And so, the defences were organised, even though the attempt was clearly so desperate as to border on madness. In this period Michelangelo was working on the Medici tombs of the New Sacristy of San Lorenzo, and he left off this work to join forces with a great architect of works of a military character, Antonio da Sangallo, so that they could collaborate on organising the fortifications for the defence of the city. Michelangelo was even appointed commissioner general of fortifications, provoking further envy and grumbling. In this capacity he was able to carry through his project for the protection of the most strategic hill of Florence: the ancient Mons Florentinum, crowned by the beautiful church of San Miniato al Monte, above the present-day Piazzale Michelangelo.

Fig. 44 - The basilica of San Miniato al Monte

On this occasion, Michelangelo also showed himself to be an ingenious military strategist. He effectively encircled the area of San Miniato with a star-shaped wall with escarpment consisting of bricks made from straw, tow (flax or hemp fibre), and horse and cow dung, which rendered the walls more elastic and better suited to soften the blows of the enemy's artillery and attenuate the rebound of the cannonballs which would have caused serious damage had the walls offered harder resistance.

The belltower of the church of San Miniato, begun by Baccio d'Agnolo and never finished, was the perfect site for an emplacement where some of the scanty Florentine artillery could be installed. But in order to protect the shaft of the belltower, which would have been an easy target for the cannon of Charles V, Michelangelo buried the lower part and covered the upper part with bales of wool and pallets filled with straw or tow – the ancestors of our modern mattresses

– creating an excellent protection against the cannon fire of the besieging army.

The story goes that, when the imperial troops came within sight of Florence, they anticipated the siege of the city by shouting 'Madonna Fiorenza, set forth your brocades that we are coming to buy them using our pikes as yardsticks'. Even the pope who, being a Medici quite legitimately considered himself a Florentine, trembled at the thought that – however much an enemy – his Florence risked suffering a siege similar to the sack that the Landsknechte had inflicted on Rome shortly before. Perhaps in his heart of hearts at that moment he repented of his agreement with Charles V and tried to save the city by sending a message to the ambassador of the republic, Bernardo da Castiglione, that if Florence would submit to him he 'would show the whole world that he was a Florentine and that he too loved his birthplace'. But it was useless: Castiglione contemptuously replied, 'Better Florence in ashes than under the Medici!'

The imperial army laid siege to the city with a massive deployment of forces, despite which every attack on the walls was promptly driven back. On their side, in a bid to break though the inflexible encirclement, the Florentines attempted the most daring surprise sorties. One of these, led by Stefano Colonna, deserves to be recounted.

Porta San Niccolò, the city gate in Piazza Giuseppe Poggi between Lungarno Serristori and Lungarno Cellini, still exists perfectly complete, a tall and solitary tower with three arches on top of each other, located below the ramps leading up to Piazzale Michelangelo. It was from this gate, one damp and foggy night, that a large group of courageous Florentines emerged, planning a surprise rearguard attack on the strong imperial position at Santa Margherita a Montici. It was pitch black and the Florentines, to avoid the risk of killing each

Fig. 45 – The belltower of San Miniato,
from the summit of which Michelangelo and Lupo fired
from culverins on the army of Charles V

other in the event of battle, had put on long white shirts over their armour. They advanced silently like ghosts in the dark night, and as they drew close to the enemy camp it seemed as though their surprise action was to be successful when fate – which on this occasion did not favour the brave – played a nasty trick on these fearless men. All of a sudden, a herd of pigs emerged from the gate of a butcher's pigsty and their squealing grunts woke up the imperial troops and gave the alarm to the entire camp.

By this stage the siege had been going on for months, and the strict encirclement began to make all its weight felt in the city. Food was running low, and with so many deaths caused by the cannon fire, the most insidious and terrible of all enemies – the plague – also made its appearance. The Florentines bravely attempted to discourage the enemy by showing all their courage – for instance on the Feast of Saint John, patron of the city, they decided to play the historic football game as usual in Piazza Santa Croce, to communicate to the besiegers that the city wasn't really that concerned about their siege. Rather, to add insult to injury, they sent several musicians up onto the roof of Santa Croce to sound their trumpets, drums and other instruments as loud as they could, expressing at full volume all their contempt for the imperial forces, while above their heads the cannonballs continued to fly.

Meanwhile, from the top of the belltower of San Miniato Michelangelo was doing his best to discommode the enemy artillery. He was assisted by a certain 'Lupo', a very courageous Florentine gunner, famous for his skill and precision in the use of cannon, mortars and culverins – an old type of cannon of small calibre and light but with a long projectile range. With the San Miniato culverins, Lupo succeeded in targeting and destroying many of the enemy cannon, also killing many of their gunners. But the enemy battalions were far too numerous and so, as we said, the actions of Michelangelo and Lupo could only be a distraction or a nuisance, and certainly not decisive for the outcome of the war.

The imbalance between the forces in the field was excessive, and the number of victims among the Florentines was vast. It is calculated that, between those killed by enemy cannon fire and in the armed clashes, combined with those who

Fig. 46 - The tower at San Niccolò

died from hunger or plague, over 44,000 citizens lost their lives in the course of the siege. The last hope of republican Florence materialised in the last-ditch attempt to obtain help from outside, and the gonfalonier managed to send a letter to this effect to the Florentine military commissioner Francesco Ferrucci, who was in Pisa, asking him to come to the aid of the city with as many men as he could muster. Ferrucci managed to cobble together a little army of 3,500 men recruited in the areas between Empoli and the Maremma, and set off with them to assist his city. However, since the recruitment of these men had perforce been effected by word of mouth, it had been impossible to avoid news of it also reaching the ears of the imperial forces. As a result, while Ferrucci was marching towards Florence, the emperor sent an army of 12,000 men under the command of the Prince of Orange to meet him, and in the end the numerical disproportion proved too great.

Francesco Ferrucci and his little army valiantly attacked the vastly greater enemy to the battle cry of the Florentine Republic 'Marzocco!' shouted with the same courageous passion with which their forbears had launched the older battle cry of 'San Giovanni!' The imperial army was taken by surprise by the onslaught, and at first it seemed that the Florentines might get the upper hand. The Prince of Orange was one of the first to fall, which discouraged the enemy and gave new hope and vigour to the Florentine soldiers. The first skirmish was won, but in the following battle of Gavinana – in which the imperial army was led by the famous Maramaldo – the Florentines took a beating and Francesco Ferrucci himself fell to the ground, badly wounded. The Florentine captain was picked up by the imperial soldiers who, seeing that he was losing a lot of blood, created a makeshift stretcher using their lances and carried him on it to their camp. Maramaldo had a particular hatred for Ferrucci and, when he learned of his presence in the camp, ordered that he should be brought before him and then gave his soldiers the order to kill him. But the soldiers considered that it was dishonourable to strike a man who was so badly wounded and refused to do it. At this, Ferruccio whipped his dagger from his belt and brought it to the throat of the by then dying man. This gesture branded Maramaldo with infamy. His name has certainly gone down in history, but only as a synonym of cowardice, as was indeed emphasised in the last words of the heroic Florentine captain who, as Maramaldo stuck the dagger into his throat, cried with his last breath: 'Coward, you strike a man who is already dead!'

That was the last armed battle for Florentine liberty: the 'Marzocco!' battle cry had echoed upon the battlefield for the survival of the Republic of Florence for the last time. The last hopes of resistance were in fact shattered by the perfidious treachery of the commander of the Florentine army, Malatesta Baglioni, who, having seen that the situation was desperate, in an attempt to personally enter the good graces of the pope, had the barefaced effrontery to order the Florentine cannon of Porta San Pietro to be turned round and directed upon the city itself!

The Republic of Florence had survived for just three years and now, under the armed guard of the victorious troops of Charles V, Florence was returned to the Medici. The end of the republic also brought to an end another glorious Florentine tradition that had survived through the centuries up to then: the florin. The beautiful gold coin that had the lily on one side and the image of St John the Baptist on the other was withdrawn from circulation and was no longer legal tender. The florin was replaced by a Medici coin designed by Benvenuto Cellini, although this never enjoyed the same success as the florin, which from then on became an object sought only by coin collectors.

In the debacle that followed the Florentine defeat, all kinds of envy, rancour and malice that had been building up deep in the hearts of many people, illustrious and not, immediately came to the surface, especially against Michelangelo and chiefly in many of his fellow artists. In this state of affairs, it was clear that if Michelangelo were to be captured his hopes of survival would have been practically non-existent. He had remained in his position at San Miniato up to the end, but when he heard that – although the Medici reinstatement had not yet taken place – they were coming after him to kill him, he took to his heels and raced down the hill, concealing himself within the tower of the Porta San Niccolò. He remained hidden there until nightfall, when he continued his flight by boat along the Arno, finally managing to leave the city, probably close to Porta Romana, and take refuge in Rome.

MICHELANGELO ACCUSED OF OBSCENITY

Pietro Aretino was an intellectual and a poet, in short, one of the most important figures among Michelangelo's contemporaries. As a writer he was irreverent, even obscene, but he was nevertheless one of the most eminent intellectuals of the time, especially in the capacity of art critic. His judgement was able to raise to the heights or cast into the abyss any artist of whom he spoke well or ill. For some time, Aretino had been putting together a private collection of works of art that he succeeded in obtaining as gifts from the leading artists of the day. Obviously, no artist would dare to deny him such a gift for fear of making an enemy of this influential figure. No one would thwart him, or rather, almost no one.

And so it happened that Aretino sent Michelangelo a letter in which he politely asked him for the gift of one of his works. However, although Michelangelo was of a very generous nature, he was certainly not the sort of man to give in to such a form of moral blackmail, so he simply ignored the letter, and also failed to reply to the other similar letters that followed. At the same time, through other channels he let it be known that, while he was grateful for Aretino's appreciation, if the latter wished to possess one of his works, he had only to purchase it. At this point, it was inevitable that Aretino began to think of a way of getting his own back on Michelangelo. He would have to act with great shrewdness, since Buonarroti was already so famous and admired that it would be impossible to attack him on his artistic merits, as he would easily have been able to do with a lesser artist.

In this period, having just narrowly escaped being killed, Michelangelo was very gloomy and downcast about the recent political events in Florence that had led to the definitive downfall of the free Florentine Republic. He was even more embittered by all the plots concocted to damage him, which among other things had obliged him to interrupt his works in San Lorenzo and flee from the city. This would also explain why, being forced to abandon the sculpture that was what he most loved doing, he decided to accept the invitation made to him by the new pope, Clement VII, to fresco the famous *Last Judgement* in the Sistine Chapel. Michelangelo worked on this masterpiece for five years, from 1536 to 1541; it was an immense labour, especially considering that he did it almost entirely on his own, practically without assistants.

It was while Michelangelo was in these conditions and in this frame of mind that the first little vendetta of Aretino arrived in the form of a letter explaining to him how he ought to arrange the *Last Judgement*; in short, a letter that implied that Michelangelo was an amateur! As we said, Michelangelo was on a particularly short fuse at the time, and on receipt of this letter he royally blew his top and immediately sat down to reply to Aretino. The tenor of his response was more or less as follows: 'Most illustrious sir, I have received your advice about how to do the *Last Judgement* and have found it to be so sound that I am convinced that, when, at the end of time, the Last Judgement shall indeed arrive, I am certain that the Eternal Father will be sure to make it happen following your wise counsel to the letter.'

We can imagine the effect of these words on Pietro Aretino and how with difficulty he managed to bottle up his rage while

174

waiting to give it full vent after Michelangelo had completed his work. He had to wait about five years, but when it came his revenge was terrible. At that point Aretino – who in all likelihood had already been working behind the scenes to create the right atmosphere – joined his voice to the rumours that had been circulating for some time, accusing Michelangelo's masterpiece of obscenity! The gist of the charge was that it was intolerable that there should be all these 'nude figures' in the Sistine Chapel, the church of the pope, and above the altar to boot. According to the accusers, the greatest disgrace of all was that it should be the great artist Michelangelo himself to conceive such obscenities. Shortly afterwards, a correspondent of the Marquis of Mantua wrote these very words: it is a 'most unseemly thing . . . to have painted so many nudes that so indecently display their shame.'

It is scarcely surprising that in this chorus of voices, that of Pietro Aretino was decisive. However, Michelangelo was saved from the most serious consequences, not so much by the prestige of his name and his artistic fame – although obviously this played an important part – but very probably by the intervention of an extremely eminent figure without links to the interested parties, who saved him from being tried and hence from an almost inevitable sentence which Aretino was counting on.

Michelangelo was indeed bound by a profound and pure friendship to Vittoria Colonna, an exquisite poet and a most noble soul, wife of the Marquis of Pescara and held in the greatest consideration by the pope and the entire Roman Curia. When this powerful woman of the strictest moral integrity took up the defence of Michelangelo, the pope dropped the legal proceedings that were being prepared against him, saving in one fell swoop Buonarroti's artistic value and his morality.

Pietro Aretino had not been expecting this turn of events and was not a little put out by it. But he did not give up and

Fig. 47 - A detail from Michelangelo's *Last Judgement*

continued to press the charge of obscenity whereby, if it was no longer possible to prosecute Michelangelo in person, then at least his works should be targeted. By this stage, the matter had become personal, and had Aretino let it drop this would certainly have damaged his own prestige. He therefore exerted all his energy and his most cunning malice until in 1564 – about one month before Michelangelo's death – the pope decided to 'dress the nudes', by having loincloths or small pieces of drapery painted in to cover the offending nudity of

176

the figures in the frescoes. This measure was, in the end, more comic than anything else, as well as being damaging to the artistic prestige of those entrusted with this thankless and far from creative task. It is probably for this very reason that the first painter assigned to executing the 'cover-ups', rather than being known by his real name, Daniele da Volterra, is instead remembered by the ridiculous nickname of 'Braghettone', or breeches-maker.

SHORT BIOGRAPHY
OF MICHELANGELO BUONARROTI

Michelangelo – or 'Michelangiolo' as he is often called in Florence – was born on 6 March 1475 in Caprese, a town not far from Chiusi della Verna, north of Arezzo. He was born in Caprese because, although his father was a Florentine, he was serving at the time as *podestà* of Caprese and Chiusi della Verna. When the Buonarroti family returned to Florence at the end of this mandate, Michelangelo was just one month old, which is why he can be considered Florentine to all effects and purposes, and he indeed defined himself as a thoroughbred Florentine. The house where he was born, in what is now called Caprese Michelangelo, still exists and has been transformed into a museum.

Michelangelo's life was as intense as it was long. He was a painter, a sculptor, an architect and even a military engineer but, as we mentioned, the form of art that he favoured above all was sculpture. Indeed, it is enough to look at the architecture of the rooms of the New Sacristy and the Biblioteca Laurenziana in San Lorenzo to realise that, more than architecture, here we are talking about 'architectural sculpture' or 'sculptural architecture'. This predilection of Michelangelo's for sculpture is confirmed by the historic documentation. In 1550, when he

Fig. 48 – Drawing showing the so-called *Rondanini Pietà*
(with the broken arm indicated by a small black arrow)

was already 75 years old and by then considered the greatest
artist of them all, he was asked to give his opinion about the
relative importance of sculpture and painting. In an autograph
letter Michelangelo replied that sculpture is superior to painting in this proportion: 'Painting is more valuable the closer it
comes to sculpture, and sculpture is less valuable the closer it
comes to painting.'

In the last years of his extremely long life, Michelangelo
was greatly attracted by the religious subject of the *Pietà*, and
he sculpted many of them, especially as his own end drew

nearer. In fact, the very last *Pietàs* had not even been commissioned by others, so that he made them for himself alone. He was fascinated by the subject – almost a return to the *Pietàs* of his youth, but with a quite different vigour – and when he died in Rome in 1564, he was working on his umpteenth and last *Pietà*: the one called the *Rondanini Pietà*, which is now in the museum of the Sforza Castle in Milan.

Michelangelo was nearly ninety years old, and yet he was still chiselling away with all the fire and passion of a youth, labouring on this beautiful work, which despite being unfinished is considered one of his finest. This magnificent *Pietà* also reveals an evident afterthought by Michelangelo who, at a certain point of the work, was no longer satisfied with the position of Christ's right arm. The artist's intention to detach the arm with blows of his chisel is clear, and he would certainly have removed it entirely had death not taken him before he could do so. And so, this arm detached from the shoulder has remained as an integral part of the sculpture, illustrating the last thoughts and the final torment of one of the greatest artists of all time.

RESEARCH SOURCES
AND HISTORIC DOCUMENTATION

- Biblioteca Nazionale di Firenze
- Various publications by Piero Bargellini
- *Storia di Firenze* by Robert Davidsohn
- *Piccola storia di Firenze* by Giovanni Spadolini
- *C'era una volta Firenze*, by Maria Bernardini
- Various Florence City Council archives
- *Antica Cronaca fiorentina* by Giovanni Villani
- *Antica Cronaca fiorentina* by Brunetto Latini
- Popular Florentine traditions

181

'NOTES AND NUMBERS ON THE MAP OF 'FLORENCE

The enclosed map of Florence shows the area inside the city ring roads, comprising practically the entire historic centre. The principal monuments mentioned in the book are marked on the map by consecutive numbers from 1 to 39.

The river Arno is marked by the letter 'A', while the main railway station of Santa Maria Novella is marked by the letter 'S'. On the map you can also see, marked by a continuous line perimeter, the part of the city that was occupied by ancient Florence at the time of its foundation in 59 BC, in which the model of the Roman castrum is easily identifiable. The city was divided into four parts by the main streets crossing it, one from north to south (the *cardo*), and the other from east to west (the

decumanus). At the precise point where these streets intersected in what is now Piazza della Repubblica, representing the exact geometrical centre, a column was erected at the time of the foundation of the city. At the top of the column was a nymph holding the cornucopia of abundance, as an augury of prosperity for *Florentia*. However, the column we see now is not the original which was corroded and ravaged by time and the elements and has been replaced several times over its history. More recently, the precise location was shifted by a few metres for reasons of traffic circulation.

The gate of the city that led from the cardo northwards (towards the Apennines and Bologna) was also known as *aquilonare* or *setten-*

trionale. Both these terms signify northern, and it is interesting to note that the term *settentrione* derives from the Latin *septem triones*, that is 'seven oxen', which is what the Latins called the seven stars of Ursa Minor, or the Little Dipper, of which the pole star is part. The streets on the map marked by long dashes interspersed with dots, and marked by numbers, show the main routes in and out of the city: no, 24 towards Rome and the south, starting from Ponte Vecchio, then Via Guicciardini and Via Senese; no. 25 towards Pisa and the sea, starting from Via Palazzuolo, then Via Il Prato and Via del Ponte alle Mosse; no. 26 towards Bologna and the north, starting from Via San Gallo, then Piazza della Libertà and Via Bolognese; no, 27 towards Casentino and Arezzo, starting from Via del Corso, then Via Pietrapiana, Via Gioberti and Via Aretina.

The oval shaped continuous line marked by no. 4 shows the perimeter of the Roman amphitheatre, one of the largest in the Roman Empire. The external curves of the walls are still easy to identify from the curved form of a good section of the streets around it – Piazza de' Peruzzi, Via Bentaccordi and Via Torta, where the houses were built on the ruins of the outer walls of the amphitheatre. For many centuries, up to the beginning of the fifteenth, Florence used the underground areas of the amphitheatre as dark dungeons in which malefactors and rebellious citizens would be locked away, along with the prisoners of war captured by the Florentine army.

The perimeter line marked with short dashes represents the wall circle of Florence at the beginning of the thirteenth century. So, even in the late mediaeval period, the main roads into and out of the city were the same as the older ones.

Instead, the perimeter marked with long dashes corresponds to the wall circle in the Renaissance, showing the enormous development of Florence over less than three centuries. In fact, at the time of Michelangelo, the walls substantially corresponded to the ring road avenues to the north of the Arno, while to the south of the river the city extended as far as the Piazzale di Porta Romana and then joined up to the east with Porta San Niccolò in Piazza Poggi.

NUMBERS

1) Position of the ancient Roman column in the centre of the city (Piazza della Repubblica)
2) Baptistery of San Giovanni Battista (Piazza San Giovanni)
3) Ponte Vecchio and the Vasari Corridor linking Palazzo Vecchio and Palazzo Pitti
4) Position of the Roman amphitheatre
5) Palazzo Vecchio, the ancient Palagio dei Priori (Piazza della Signoria)
6) Church of the Badia Fiorentina (Via del Proconsolo)
7) Palazzo del Bargello, now national museum (Via del Proconsolo)
8) Santa Maria del Fiore: the Cathedral of Florence (Piazza del Duomo)
9) Basilica of San Lorenzo, Medici Chapels and Biblioteca Laurenziana (Piazza San Lorenzo)
10) Palazzo Medici Riccardi, which was the home of the Medici family (Via Cavour)
11) Complex of the Basilica of the Santissima Annunziata and the Ospedale degli Innocenti (Piazza Santissima Annunziata)
12) Ospedale di Santa Maria Nuova (Piazza Santa Maria Nuova)
13) Synagogue (Via Farini)
14) Basilica of Santa Croce and Pazzi Chapel (Piazza Santa Croce)
15) Tower of San Niccolò (Piazza Poggi)
16) Church of Santo Spirito (Piazza Santo Spirito)
17) Palazzo Corsini (Via del Parione)
18) Palazzo Strozzi (Piazza Strozzi)
19) Church of Ognissanti (Piazza Ognissanti)
20) Church of Santa Maria Novella (Piazza Santa Maria Novella)
21) Uffizi Gallery, Loggia della Signoria, Loggiato of the Uffizi (Piazzale degli Uffizi)
22) Porta al Prato (Piazzale di Porta al Prato)
23) Fortezza da Basso (Viale Filippo Strozzi)
24) Old road towards Rome and the south
25) Old road towards Pisa, Lucca and the sea
26) Old road towards Bologna and the north
27) Old road towards Casentino and Arezzo
28) Ponte alla Carraia
29) Ponte alle Grazie
30) Church of Santo Stefano al Ponte (Piazza Santo Stefano)
31) Church of Sant'Ambrogio (Piazza Sant'Ambrogio)
32) Orsanmichele (Via dei Calzaioli)
33) Torre della Zecca (Piazza Piave)
34) Convent and Museum of San Marco (Piazza San Marco)
35) Ponte Santa Trinita
36) Galleria dell'Accademia di Belle Arti, where the original of Michelangelo's *David* is displayed (Via Ricasoli)
37) House of Giovanni da Verrazzano. In the same street, Via Giovanni da Verrazzano, is the plaque set up by an old Florentine who went to Rome with his wife for the Jubilee of 1300
38) Palazzo Pitti, which was the home of the last Medici, later becoming a royal palace when Florence was the capital of Italy (Piazza de' Pitti)
39) Palazzo Rucellai (Via della Vigna Nuova)

A) River Arno
S) Santa Maria Novella railway station (Piazza della Stazione)

184

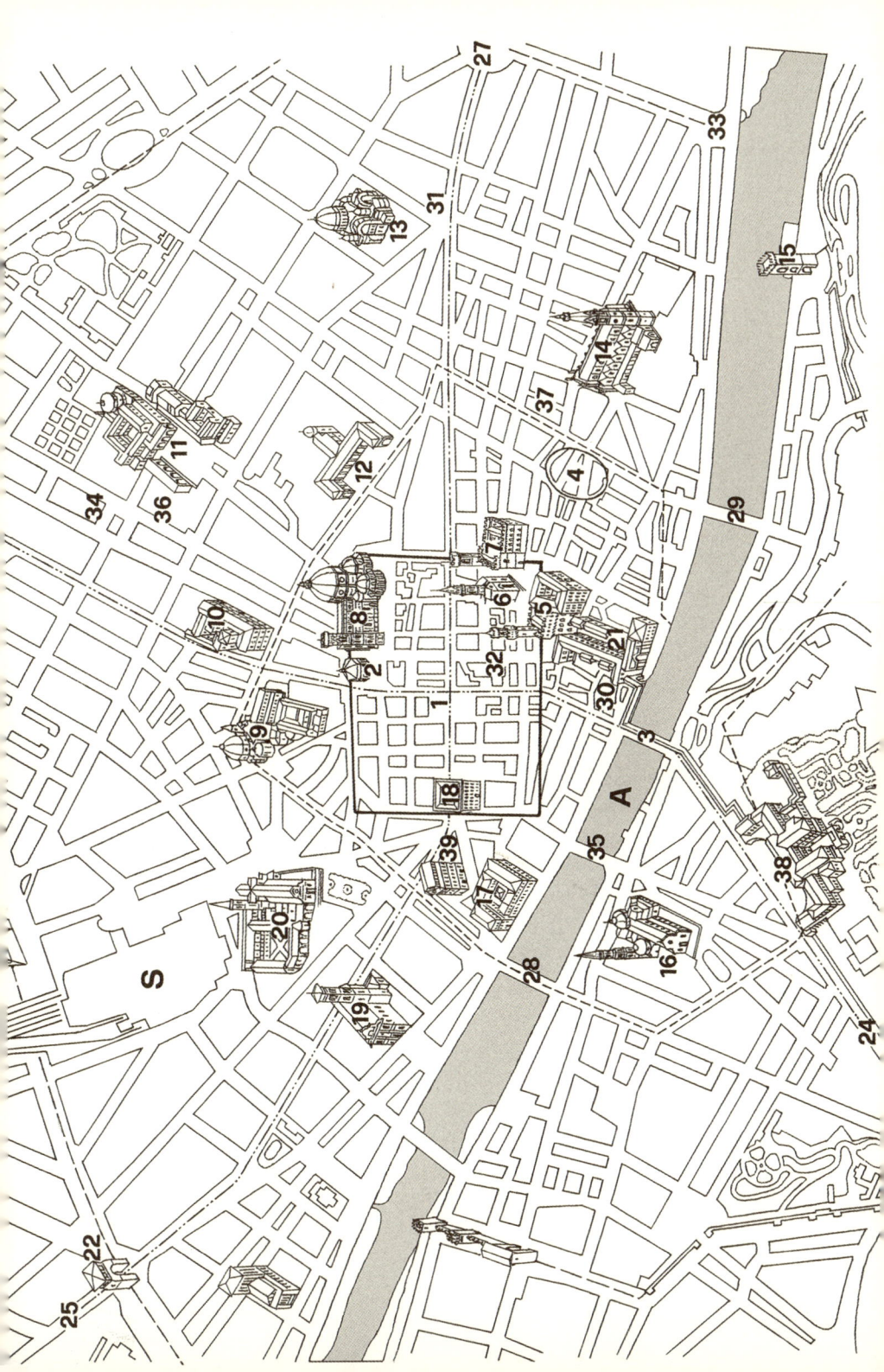

INDEX OF ILLUSTRATIONS

INDEX

Printed at
POLISTAMPA FIRENZE srl
January 2025